Fr. Benedict Answers Your Questions

Fr. Benedict Groeschel, C.F.R.

Fr. Benedict Answers Your Questions

EWTN Publishing, Inc.
Irondale, Alabama

The questions and answers in this book are
based on EWTN's *Sunday Night Live*.

Cover design by LUCAS Art & Design, Jenison, MI.

On the cover: Retro TV set (HDBKCD)
© Maksym Yemelyanov / Alamy Stock Photo.

EWTN Publishing, Inc.
5817 Old Leeds Road, Irondale, AL 35210

Distributed by
Sophia Institute Press, Box 5284, Manchester, NH 03108

paperback ISBN 978-1-68278-279-8

ebook ISBN 978-1-68278-280-4

Library of Congress Control Number: 2023930193

First printing

Contents

Introduction 1
Abortionists. 3
Addiction and Death 5
Adoration 8
The Age of the Earth 9
Apparitions 12
Attacks on the Catholic Church 14
Baptismal Efficacy. 17
Beards 20
The Blessed Mother 21
Canonization of Same-Sex Persons? 23
Catholic Education: Evaluation of Catholic Schools 25
Catholic Education: Violations of Catholic Teaching 27
Censoring Christmas 30
Chastity 31
Church and State 33
Confession: Why Must We Confess? 36
Confession: Making a Good One 38
Conversion and the Family's Reaction 40
The Coptic Tradition 41
A Course in Miracles 44
Criticizing the Pope 47
The Crucifix 51
Crucifixes with the Resurrected Jesus 53
Cults: Freedom for a Former Member 55
The Da Vinci Code. 57
Death Experience of Fr. Groeschel 59

Depression 62
Divine Mercy and St. Faustina 64
Divorce 66
The Disciples' "Doubt" 68
End-of-Life Decisions 70
Eternal Life 71
An Evangelical Ex-Catholic: In Danger? 75
Evil Influence 76
The Faith of Non-Christians 80
Fanaticism 82
Fatherhood and Abuse 84
Forgiveness and Reconciliation 87
Forgiveness in the Face of Defiance 90
Forgiveness of Self 93
The Franciscan Way and Corruptions of It 96
Free Will 98
Gnostic Gospels 100
God's Name: The Secular Banishment of It 103
God's Will and Spiritual Warfare 105
Grief: The Death of One's Spouse 109
Religious Habits 111
Head Coverings 115
The Hippopotamus 117
Historical Reliability of the Catholic Faith 120
History and Biblical Scholarship 124
Holy Communion: Exclusion of Non-Catholic Christians 126
Holy Communion: Guidance for a Lutheran 128
Holy Communion: Partaking under One Species 130
Holy Communion: Receiving More Than Once a Day 132

Holy Communion: Receiving Worthily 133
Holy Communion: Reverence for It 137
The Holy Spirit 139
The Human Body Glorified 141
Humility: Genuine 143
Illegal Immigration 145
The Image of God 149
The *In Paradisum* Prayer 151
Jesus' Divinity. 152
Jesus: Resurrected and Unrecognized 156
Jesus' Healings: Why Did He Try to Keep Them Quiet? 158
Job Situation: Hostile Boss 159
Life after Prison 161
Liturgical "Collapse" 163
Liturgy: Participation of the Laity 165
Lourdes 167
"Marriage" for Homosexuals 169
Masons 171
Mass Intentions. 174
Mass Obligation 177
Mother Elvira 180
Mother Teresa and Princess Diana 182
Muslims. 184
"Only Son of God" 186
Original Sin. 188
The Orthodox Church 191
The Poem of the Man-God and Private Revelation 193
The Pope and the People 194
Prayer and God's Answer 196

Prayer Requests 200
Prayer: Intercessory Value for the Dead. 201
Prayer and Thinking 203
Priests: How to Encourage Them. 206
Priests: When They Are in Error 209
Private Revelations 212
Psychological Examinations for Priests and Religious 215
Purgatory: Is It Biblical?. 216
Purgatory: Is It a Metaphor? 220
Purgatory: St. Catherine of Genoa,
St. John Henry Newman, and *Spe Salvi* 223
Purity: How to Cultivate It in the World. 228
Religions: Christian and Non-Christian 230
Religious Orders 232
The Resurrection: Did Jesus Visit His Mother?. 234
Returning to the Church 235
Satan: Should We Hate Him?. 237
Scripture and Speculation 238
Service and Suffering 241
Sin against the Holy Spirit 244
Sin: Speaking Clearly about It 245
Suicide 246
Theodicy: God's Justice and Human Suffering. 248
Thomas à Kempis's Death 250
Translation of Prayers. 252
Tridentine Mass. 254
Unbelief and Church Membership 257
The Vocation Crisis. 261
Women Priests?. 263

Introduction

Fr. Benedict Groeschel, C.F.R. (1933–2014) was a priest, psychologist, and co-founder of the Franciscan Friars of the Renewal. The many hats he wore in his vocation as a Franciscan friar were especially apparent when he hosted *Sunday Night Live* and when he was a frequent guest of Mother Angelica on EWTN over the years.

The bearded friar was known for his role as a teacher, especially on spiritual retreats and in college classrooms, as well as for his efforts on behalf of the poor of New York City. Like Fulton J. Sheen, Fr. Groeschel taught lessons about the Faith that were within the grasp of his audience, and his words remain both orthodox and full of love and understanding. He was director of Trinity Retreat House in Larchmont, New York; taught pastoral psychology at St. Joseph's Seminary in Dunwoodie; founded St. Francis House and Good Counsel Homes; and served as chaplain at Children's Village in Dobbs Ferry.

Fr. Groeschel hosted more than three hundred episodes of *Sunday Night Live* and multiple other EWTN TV series. Throughout these shows, Father would take questions on just about every subject and often took questions from the audience. Viewers from across the world mailed and e-mailed questions to the studio to hear Fr. Groeschel's thoughts. These letter writers asked about a range of topics, including questions about faith, doctrine, mental health, and modern controversies.

This book collects more than a hundred of these questions and the answers from Fr. Benedict Groeschel. Each chapter is presented alphabetically by subject so you can easily find answers to questions you may have (or will have) about Catholicism.

As a priest and a Franciscan friar, Fr. Groeschel showed a pastoral ability to explain the truths of Catholicism to a wide audience. He also answered questions by drawing on his work as a psychologist, teacher, pro-life activist, and religious-community founder.

Fr. Groeschel's answers to 114 of these questions are now before you in this book. This is a gift, both from Father and from God, who preserved Fr. Benedict's life. "The Providence of God," he would often say, "was the mystery of God reaching out at every moment and revealing His love and presence to us all."

Fr. Benedict passed away on October 3, 2014, the vigil of the feast of St. Francis.

Abortionists

I know you are not only a priest but also a psychologist, so I wanted to ask you: What is the psychology of an abortionist? How is one able to kill people for a living?

The human mind is equipped with various defenses, classically called *defense mechanisms*, that cause us to think of "good reasons" for doing bad things or bad reasons for not doing anything, and one of the great defenses is *denial*. Denial is the pretense that reality is different from what it actually is.

You could ask the same question about the men who ran the Auschwitz concentration camp. The Nazis did open the prisons and let some psychopaths into the SS,[1] but, as several writers—especially Hannah Arendt—have pointed out, there were also schoolteachers, plumbers, and bakers who were drafted into the SS. The Nazis convinced them that they were victims and that Jews and others were not human beings. Some otherwise ordinary people began to believe it. A Polish priest friend of mine who spent four and a half years in Auschwitz and Dachau told me many stories; for example, how they could convince the SS that their prisoners were

1 *Schutzstaffel*, which means "protection echelon": a unit of Nazis created as a bodyguard for Hitler.

subhuman. Occasionally, however, it would break through their minds that these prisoners were human beings. It happened once that an SS guard saved the life of my friend. He said to another SS guard who was torturing my friend, “Don’t you realize this is a human being?” No, that guard did not.

Those abortionists and their assistants and supporters who, when you meet them in society, are very nice people, are in denial. They clearly think they’re doing something good, but in reality, what they are doing is denying what they intellectually must admit—namely, that the unborn child is a human being. This is very dangerous because soon we will be convincing ourselves that the elderly, the physically handicapped, and the mentally ill are not human beings either.

Addiction and Death

My sister recently died suddenly at only forty-five years of age. She was a drug addict, and we believe that she accidentally overdosed and did not intend to kill herself. However, I would like to know how the Church would view her death. Though she did die from her own action, she got the drugs from a dealer. What would be her sin? "Thou shalt not kill," says the Lord our God. She was confirmed in the Catholic Church but did not practice the Faith.

Many people are concerned about the salvation of someone dear to them, living or deceased. What you must do is *put it into the hands of God*. Years ago, the Church, seeking to discourage suicide, would not let a suicide be buried in the Church. The priest had to say the prayers in the funeral parlor, and Mass couldn't be offered for the person. But in the last fifty years, there has been a much greater understanding of human psychology and a recognition that many people who take their own lives are not responsible for what they do. Thank God for that, because it is a tragedy for the members of their families. I myself lived through the suicide of a young fellow who was in our home for boys in Brooklyn. I was very consoled to be able to offer his funeral Mass amid that great sorrow.

Moreover, when a person has been pulled into something terribly destructive, such as drug addiction, there must be other problems, other cracks in the personality. I'm very convinced that, for people who die because their lives were messed up by addiction, often enough there were many extenuating circumstances that would make it more understandable to us. But none of us can judge someone else.

What about God? Remember the revelation of Divine Mercy to St. Faustina. Christ revealed to her that He calls to every soul in the hour of death and that He doesn't call just once but three times.[2] This is a mystical number, meaning insistence. Christ insists. St. Faustina also made it clear that Christ told her that the soul is ultimately free. It must choose the Divine Mercy. But St. Faustina described it in such a way that if the dying soul rejects the Divine Mercy, the Divine Mercy doesn't give up. It pursues the soul, looking for its freedom.

Now, you might ask me where something like that is in the Scripture. Good question. And we have a very interesting example: the death of the good thief. This thief, crucified with Christ, said that he himself was guilty and deserved it. He said to Christ, "Remember me when you come into your kingly power." And Christ said to him, "Today you will be with me in Paradise." (Luke 23:42–43). How many of us, even if we're very well-behaved Christians, would dare to say that we lead a good Christian life because of our own decisions, because of our own strength? That would be a horrible thing for a Christian to say or think. St. Teresa of Ávila once said that she prayed for Judas. People were shocked. How could you pray for Judas? She said, "I pray that he repented in the moment of death." But why? Why would you pray for Judas? He betrayed Christ! And St. Teresa looked at them and said, "So did I, but I

2 *Diary of Saint Maria Faustina Kowalska: Divine Mercy in My Soul*, no. 1486.

have hope of salvation." Never give up on anybody. As it says in the Old Testament, "His mercy endures forever" (Ps. 136, NABRE). The Latin is very beautiful: *Quoniam in aeternum misericordia eius.*

So let's always proceed with great confidence in the mercy of God.

Adoration

Father, can you tell me what spiritual benefits I receive from spending time in adoration of the Lord during a holy hour?

First, it's a great idea to be so obviously and consciously in the presence of the Son. Now, we know that Christ is, in a very real way, everywhere, because He's the Word of God, Who holds all things in existence. We know that through Him all things where made. But in the Eucharist, in His Body and Blood, you have a mystical, incomprehensible, mysterious presence, not only of the Eternal Word of God, the second Person of the Blessed Trinity, but of Christ Jesus of Nazareth, the Son of Mary. St. Francis understood this and received immense strength and courage and blessings from adoration. Our dear Mother [now St.] Teresa in our own time said that without the Holy Eucharist, she would stumble and fall. Her advice was to spend an hour every day in the presence of Christ, and you will change for the better. You may not change too obviously, but while you're kneeling there and praying, your life will come before you, and you will see things in a different way, and maybe you will begin to see things as He sees them.

The Age of the Earth

How old is our earth? I know that talk about millions and billions of years is just a guess, or is it?

First, the Bible is not written as a scientific book, and people even knew that in ancient times. So when Genesis 1 speaks of the six days of creation, people in ancient times knew that didn't mean twenty-four-hour days. I'll give you an example: St. Augustine, writing in his book called *The Literal Meaning of the Book of Genesis*, says that perhaps the six days means six years, or maybe it means sixty years, or maybe it means six hundred years. Or maybe it means six thousand years. Or maybe it means six hundred thousand years, and maybe it means six hundred thousand times six hundred thousand years, which is interesting because that comes out to about three and a half billion. St. Augustine was making guesses without any scientific knowledge at all; he was just preaching.

Scientists estimate that the earth is about 4.5 billion years old. I had nothing to do with that calculation. It was calculated by geologists and other scientists, based largely on the decomposition of fissionable atomic materials in rocks. I'm perfectly willing to accept it because Genesis can't mean to indicate that the earth is six thousand years old. Further, there is no reason to adopt a narrow definition of "days." For God "one day is as a thousand years and a thousand years as one day" (2 Pet. 3:8).

The universe itself is thought to be quite a bit older than the earth, and they seem to keep changing the estimate, so I'm a little bit hesitant to say: sometimes I read eleven billion years old, sometimes fourteen billion. I wasn't there, of course; I'm involved only with the last seventy years! It is quite remarkable and important to know that, in Genesis 1, the order of creation—light, space, the sea, the land, the creatures in the sea, the animals, and then man—follows the same pattern we arrive at in science and paleontology and natural history: that we got the animals before the people. And I think that's a rather beautiful thing.

Also, the big bang theory, which says that the entire universe originated with a very small object and then exploded, originated with the work of two scientists working contemporaneously: Edwin Hubble and Georges Lemaître. Rarely do they tell you that Lemaître was a Jesuit priest and a close friend of Einstein. I have a picture of Lemaître, wearing his Roman collar, talking to Einstein, who liked to talk to priests. The big bang theory was in and out of favor for a long time and is now generally the scientific consensus. Pope Pius XII observed that it fit well with the biblical idea of creation.[3]

Now they're hypothesizing about a "planck"[4] particle, a tiny black hole one-millionth the size of a proton, which is itself a tiny particle that is part of an atom. The philosophical definition of creation and the theological definition is "being from nothing,"

3 Pope Piux XII, "Proofs for the Existence of God in Light of Modern Natural Science" (November 22, 1951), EWTN, https://www.ewtn.com/catholicism/library/proofs-for-the-existence-of-god-in-the-light-of-modern-natural-science-8950.

4 Named for Max Planck (1858–1947), the German theoretical physicist who originated quantum theory.

and so if you get down to a planck, it's being from next to nothing. That's why I love astronomy, and I particularly love *God and the Astronomers*,[5] by Robert Jastrow, former head of the NASA Space Laboratories and professor emeritus of astronomy at Columbia.

5 Robert Jastrow, *God and the Astronomers*, 2nd ed. (New York: Reader's Library, Inc., 1992).

Apparitions

I heard that there were around fifty false apparitions that sprang up around the country in 1958. How would you respond to the movement of people who chase apparitions?

I've done a book on this, which some of you may be familiar with. It's called *A Still Small Voice: A Practical Guide on Reported Revelations.*[6] It presents the Church's official teaching on private revelations. The first thing to know is that it can be a violation of the first commandment to go around proclaiming, without sufficient reason, that a private revelation has been made. Sufficient reason includes at least the approval of the diocesan bishop. This does not mean that an interested person could not say that such a report sounds as if it *might be* a private revelation. That would not be a violation of the commandment. But to announce that the Blessed Mother appeared in Canarsie[7] when you know nothing about it except by rumor: that is improper and could be a sin.

People look for private revelations because of the theological and moral shakiness of the world in which we live. Certain

[6] Benedict J. Groeschel, *A Still Small Voice: A Practical Guide on Reported Revelations* (San Francisco: Ignatius Press, 1993).

[7] A neighborhood in Brooklyn.

theologians dismiss fundamental dogmatic and moral teachings of the Church, and so people look for a "fifth gospel," another revelation. This is not wise. I don't blame the people shaken by our theological climate for looking for a fifth revelation beyond the four Gospels. I blame the irresponsible writers and scholars. But it is important to remember that the revelation given to us in sacred Scripture is complete. St. John of the Cross, the greatest mystical writer of the Catholic Church, puts into the mouth of God these words: "I have given you everything. I have given you My beloved Son, listen to Him." If there is a private revelation, it can only be used to emphasize and bring to bear on a particular moment in history what we already know from Sacred Scripture.

Attacks on the Catholic Church

In early November, Archbishop Dolan made a severe criticism of the New York Times, *and especially of an editorial writer named Maureen Dowd. He accused the people at the* New York Times *of promoting prejudice and printing false information on the Catholic Church. This attack on the Church is continuing. What should we do in response to this attack, especially because the* New York Times, *although diminished, still has a share of influence in the media?*

Those of you who are not living in the New York area and not reading the *Times* may not know that there is a relentless attack on the Catholic Church, particularly in its editorials, and particularly by Ms. Dowd, who claims to have gone to Catholic school. We in the archdiocese of New York and in the Church are able to put up with a lot of criticism, but this is vicious and angry. If somebody wants to be vicious and angry about the Church, that's their business, but it does not belong in the media. Archbishop [now Cardinal] Dolan wrote a letter in response, which the *New York Times* refused to publish as an editorial. Dolan then published it on his blog, and it was picked up by some of the other New York newspapers.[8] In it,

[8] The *New York Times* offered to post Archbishop [now Cardinal] Dolan's reply as a letter to the editor, but he refused because of the

he pointed out the *Times*'s relentless bigotry against the Church. You might ask how somebody could be a bigot if she was already a Catholic [referring to Maureen Dowd]. There are many different views within the Church, and people can express their belief or disagreement in decent ways, in sharp ways, and even in vicious ways. When it's vicious, it's very unfortunate. I've been reading the *Times* for sixty-five years. When I was a kid, we always called it "the Grey Lady." I've been reading it all my life, but in recent years, it has been become consistently anti-Catholic. In many ways, it has become consistently anti-religion, and, unfortunately, it's getting worse and worse.

The questioner mentioned that the *New York Times* is "diminishing." There are a lot of people who will not read it. A great many of my Jewish friends have told me that the *Times* has shown a prejudice against the state of Israel, and for that reason, they will not read it. My own doctor stopped reading the *Times* years ago. So we're not the only people, and it's unfortunate that this newspaper, which they call "the newspaper of record," is going to be deprived of all of us. At our retreat house, we recently canceled our subscription, and we've selected another New York newspaper that is sober, serious, and intellectual. I don't always agree with that newspaper either, but it does give us an alternative. It's particularly unfortunate that the *Times* could be so very biased against the pro-life movement. It is pro-abortion.

---

routine practice of condensing letters to the editor, which would pose a risk of losing or neutering his major points. The particular blog to which the archbishop posted his letter is no longer active. The text of the October 29, 2009, letter can be read at the following link: https://the-american-catholic.com/2009/10/30/new-york-times-rejects-archbishop-dolans-article-why/.

Moreover, during the Vietnam War, I was in the peace movement because I thought we should get out of Vietnam. The *Times* really was prejudiced against the peace movement in their news reporting. They are entitled to their prejudices, and if they want to write them on the editorial page, that's their business. But when you put the editorials on the news page, then that's dishonest. I'm hoping and praying that the Grey Lady will get converted, because right now, we all think she's become a grey witch. I would like to see the *Times* change, and I hope that the Sulzberger family, which has owned it for many years, will listen to people like me and many others.

Baptismal Efficacy

I was baptized in a Protestant church that didn't believe that Baptism was a cleansing in any way, that it was just a public statement of faith. I am now in RCIA and getting close to the sacrament of Reconciliation. Was I truly baptized if there was no intention of cleansing my sins?

The basic teaching of the theologians, which is followed by the Church as a practice, is that a baptism is valid when the one who baptizes does so with the intention of doing what Christ wanted when He commanded His disciples to go and baptize all nations (see Matt. 28:19). Now, there are some Protestant churches that do not accept that teaching. That rejection of Catholic teaching came out of the Reformation, and some believed that the person who baptized you had to be a devout Christian. But the fact is that this Protestant understanding disagrees with the practice of the early Church.

This question brings out the different understandings of Baptism and the sacraments from the Catholic and the Orthodox churches on one side and some—not all—of the Protestant churches on the other side. Generally, Anglicans and Lutherans would side with the Catholics on this issue, though there is some disagreement within those bodies on this issue. In the very early Church, this question came up: Could a pagan baptize somebody in a case of necessity? You might ask, “What might that necessity be?” Suppose two people are in a prison cell, and they’re both going to get thrown to the lions. One of them is a Christian, and the other is a pagan. But the Christian hasn’t been baptized yet. He’s a catechumen; he has been getting ready for Baptism. Can he ask the pagan to baptize him? The answer in the early Church was *yes*, if the pagan did what he was supposed to do: pour the water over the head of the person; say the words “I baptize you in the name of the Father and of the Son and of the Holy Spirit”; and intend to do what Jesus had commanded. If all this was satisfied, then the person was baptized. Now, admittedly, he might feel a little uncomfortable, but he’d be baptized because in the early Church, as in the Catholic and Orthodox churches today, it is Christ who baptizes. He is the one who gives you His Body and Blood. He is the one who absolves your sins in Confession. He is the one who gives the sacrament. The minister, the priest, is just the instrument of Christ.

Baptism began to be understood by some of the early Protestant churches as a confession of faith and the acceptance of Christ as one’s Savior. The Protestants, having changed the definition of *sacrament*, emphasized the human side of the sacraments. Now, Christ is the author of Baptism, and He baptizes. We priests stand in for Him, and consequently, when a person is properly baptized, I accept that, because whoever baptized that person was intending to do what Christ did. People have been known merely to simulate Baptism. For instance, in Nazi Germany, some Jewish people were “baptized” without intending to become Christians, in order to fool the Nazis. Those baptisms are not valid. They didn’t intend it as anything other than a ruse. So the mere act of baptism does not make you a Christian. There must be intent to become what Christ wants a person to become in Baptism. Even a pagan, if he were to baptize, must intend to do what Christ intended.

As I said, many Protestants don't understand sacraments as Catholic and Orthodox Christians do. Sacraments, for us, are mysteries. What is a mystery? Einstein said that a mystery is something that you perceive but find incomprehensible. That's what we say: the mystery of Baptism, to take away the sins of a person; the mystery of the Eucharist; the mystery of the absolution of sin. All this is mysterious. But among the Protestant churches, particularly the Reformed churches, which trace their origin to Ulrich Zwingli, many do not have the same idea of a sacrament.

Beards

Fr. Benedict, why do you wear a beard?

First, I wear a beard because I don't shave! But in our Franciscan community, the beard is a custom, and many of the friars wear great big beards. Compared with other friars, I have a somewhat small beard. This custom goes back to our origins in the Order of Capuchins, who always wore beards in the old days. In fact, the great composer Mozart wrote a beautiful little four-part motet, in four voices, *Venerabilis Barba Capucinorum*, "To the venerable beard of the Capuchins."

So, why do we wear beards? Most importantly, it reminds people of Jesus. Secondly, it means that we don't have to take such good care of ourselves. When I come on the program, Lillian, who is also usually in the audience, trims my beard, making it look much more pleasant, and puts on the makeup so I don't look like I'm dying on the set.

The Blessed Mother

Mary calls herself the Immaculate Conception and the Lady of the Rosary. But what is the significance of the many other titles we use for the Blessed Mother, and who approves them? For example, Our Lady of Mercy, Our Lady of Perpetual Help, Our Lady of Sorrows, Our Lady of the Snows, Our Lady Queen of Peace, Our Lady of Victory, Our Lady of the Sacred Heart, et cetera.

You will find, if you sit down and research these various titles, that they're often related to some historical event. For example, Our Lady of Victory comes from the miraculous Christian naval victory at the Battle of Lepanto, after those on the Christian side invoked the Virgin Mary and prayed the Rosary. You'll also find that there are beautiful legends about certain titles, such as Our Lady of the Snows. The legend is that a Roman patrician who had no heirs had vowed to donate his property to the Virgin Mary. He and his wife prayed for a sign to show them how they might dispose of the money, and on August 5, in the middle of the summer, snow fell on the summit of the Esquiline Hill. They therefore built there a great church in honor of Our Lady.

These are different titles that arise in all different ways, and they need the approval, at least, of a diocesan bishop. So nobody should make up titles on their own. My favorite is Our Lady of

Sorrows, because for all us, life has many sorrows. And as you may remember in the film *The Passion of the Christ*, it was brought out so beautifully that Our Lady was in the greatest of sorrows as she attended the death of her beloved Son.[9] So we can all be consoled by that title.

[9] See Simeon's words to Mary in Luke 2:34-36.

Canonization of Same-Sex Persons?

Will the Catholic Church ever recognize a person with same-sex attraction as a saint, if they met all the requirements for canonization that the Church sets forth and lived according to all the Church's teachings. If not, could you explain?

The answer is, of course. Regardless of what their difficulties may be, anyone who leads a holy, chaste, and virtuous life, and who does so in a heroic way can be canonized. Having worked with many people with same-sex attractions, I know that some of them lead very chaste lives. Some of them very seriously struggle to do that and, for the most part, succeed; some don't try, but think about trying. I have never met anybody who decided beforehand that they wanted to have this difficulty. It does seem, though, that it offers an opportunity for heroic virtue, and heroic virtue is what makes a saint. We're all supposed to be virtuous, but saints are virtuous when it's heroic to be so, and many people leading chaste lives with same-sex attraction do practice heroic virtue, at least in that particular category.

Let me tell you a story. I was at the annual Courage[10] convention, and I was driven to the airport by a young man in his twenties

[10] Courage International is a Catholic ministry that assists people who experience same-sex attraction to live chaste lives.

who belongs to Courage in a small city where there is just one Courage group. He also belongs to Sexaholics Anonymous. He explained to me that he cannot hang out with all the people who are struggling to find the right spouse and get married and are appropriately dating; and he can't hang out in what they call the gay scene because those people aren't trying to be chaste. So, his social circle is made up, for the most part, of people with same-sex attractions who are trying to lead chaste lives. In that small city, it's a very small number of people. I told him that I have the greatest admiration for his courage and sincerity and that God will surely reward him for his heroic efforts.

As I'm answering this question, I want to encourage people with same-sex attractions to have as good a social life as possible, while preserving their chastity and supporting one another. I encourage you also to be perfectly at home with other people who don't have this difficulty. People who have heterosexual attractions have difficulties too, and they must behave themselves. Finally, I encourage people who have same-sex attraction to join with others, either through Courage, which is a Catholic ministry, or Exodus, which is an Evangelical Protestant ministry. We all need to have support from other people, and when we have it, we do better. I wouldn't be the slightest bit surprised if, in the Litany of the Saints, more than once, without knowing it, you have invoked the name of a saint who, in their lifetime, struggled with same-sex attraction.

Catholic Education: Evaluation of Catholic Schools

What is a good source to evaluate Catholic colleges and schools?

It is very important to evaluate them. I worked with the Cardinal Newman Society, which encourages authentic Catholic higher education and publishes a guide to faithful Catholic colleges.[11] We evaluated Catholic colleges on the following criteria: (1) genuine teaching of the Catholic Faith as guided by the Holy Father and the Tradition of the Church; (2) the moral climate of the school—what it tolerates, what it permits; (3) whether the college observes Pope John Paul II's apostolic constitution *Ex Corde Ecclesiae*, "From the Heart of the Church," which requires a commitment on the part of those who teach theology to teach *authentic* Catholic theology. Unfortunately, not many fulfilled all those requirements. We have about twenty-one colleges in the present list[12] out of two hundred Catholic colleges in this country, which is tragic. There were a number that were, say, three-quarters of the way there, and one

[11] "Recommended Colleges for Catholic Families" (cardinalnewmansociety.org/the-newman-guide/).

[12] This is as of 2008. In 2022, the Newman Guide recommends nineteen American colleges and six international colleges.

or two with serious glaring defects. The others were totally off the boards, such that seemingly nothing short of the Last Judgment will ever bring them around to being considered an authentic Catholic college.

It's also important, whether you're looking at a college or a high school, to find out what the climate is. Years ago, you didn't have to do this with Catholic schools, but now people take the name "Catholic" very lightly, so find out what's going on at the school. Be snoopy. And ask some people whose opinions you value, particularly clergy who may be informed about a particular school. Several bishops in the United States have openly criticized Catholic colleges in their dioceses for various misbehavior. Others haven't been criticized yet, but they ought to be criticized.

On several occasions, a parent has told me that a child has lost faith after having been sent to a Catholic college. Sadly, given the colleges their children went to, I could have told those parents that that was very likely to happen. One of our sisters went to Boston College, and she told me that she was put into the position of constantly having to defend Catholic teaching in class. She wrote a long explanation and description of what she went through, and when I sent it to the major superiors of the Society of Jesus, I received a discourteous and dismissive letter in return.

So be careful, and *don't be bullied.*

Catholic Education: Violations of Catholic Teaching

If a student finds herself enrolled in a supposed Catholic college where there are clear violations of Catholic teaching in the classroom and/or in campus life, what response is appropriate for that student and the student's parents? Should letters be written to the local bishop?

If you find yourself in a college that calls itself Catholic but allows heretical teachings and public immorality, encourages immorality in dormitory setups, and disparages the Catholic Faith to the point of inviting onto the campus speakers who are hostile toward the Catholic Church, then you're in a phony Catholic college. The College of the Holy Cross in Worcester, Massachusetts, once sponsored an event in which they invited a couple of major pro-abortion organizations to participate. This is absolutely scandalous. My uncle, who at age nineteen was the youngest graduate of Holy Cross College and who went on to become an extremely successful physician, would be absolutely appalled to know this about his alma mater.

In any case, a college or university that calls itself Catholic is responsible to the bishop of the diocese not to give scandal and false teaching. I wrote to the Congregation for Catholic Education[13]

[13] Now the Dicastery for Culture and Education.

about some outrageous things that one of our sisters experienced at Boston College. I was told by the congregation to refer this to the local bishop, who had responsibility to correct them. Unfortunately, the local bishop, Cardinal O'Malley, was not able to do so. But I'm happy to say that, in the case of Holy Cross, the local bishop, Robert McManus, let them know that they had crossed the line. He may not have had any legal standing to do anything, and if so, that is unfortunate.

Some years ago, a group of college presidents, led, unfortunately, by the famous Fr. Hesburgh[14] of Notre Dame University, met at a conference in Land O' Lakes, Wisconsin, where they signed what is known as the Land O' Lakes Statement, which effectively moved Catholic higher education out of any real jurisdiction of the Church and the hierarchy. Though they thought they were doing good, they did a tremendous disservice to Catholic higher education, which I think is presently generally in a state of apostasy. This is no slight matter, because the charter on which Catholic education or Christian education stands consists of the words of our Lord Jesus Christ. At the very end of His earthly stay, He commanded His disciples, "Go therefore and make disciples of all nations, baptizing them in the name of the Father and of the Son and of the Holy Spirit, teaching them to observe all that I have commanded you" (Matt. 28:19–20). Either they believe that, or they don't. They either must admit that they're failing, or they should tell us all that they don't believe it.

Back to the question: I would write first to the president of the college, outlining carefully, succinctly, and particularly the serious violations of Catholic Faith and teaching you've encountered at the

[14] Fr. Theodore Hesburgh, C.S.C., was president of the University of Notre Dame from 1957 until 1982.

college. Name it; put it down in writing. If you don't know how to write the letter, get a lawyer friend of yours to help you write it. It's an indictment. You will probably get no answer or perhaps some kind of a silly answer from the dean that just tells you to be a good fellow, be a good girl, and sit over in the corner and keep your mouth shut because we all know much more than you do. I've received these kinds of demeaning responses. When that comes, then you write to the bishop and put the whole thing in front of him and see what he can or will do. And I would keep going: if the bishop feels he can do only so much, then write to the [Dicastery for Culture and Education] in Rome. But if the college is run by a Catholic religious order, write first to the provincial of that order, and then to the father general, and then to the Dicastery in Rome. Send them the facts; let it be known.

These are unbiased opinions, you know, just very gently expressed, and I hope you don't get too mad at me!

Censoring Christmas

Soon we will be coming into the Christmas season. Last year, the stores tried very hard to avoid mentioning the word Christmas. *What should we do?*

I would speak to your friendly local department store, supermarket, anything else, and tell them right now that if they leave the word *Christmas* out of their appeal for people to buy things during the Christmas season, if they forbid Christmas, if they ignore Christmas, you will not buy from them. If there are many stores like that, I suggest that parishes have gift fairs where people donate lots of items so that others can buy their presents in the church. I plan to do a big show on this, and I'm going to give out the annual Ebenezer Scrooge Awards to those big chains of stores that outlaw Christmas. This is an outrage.

And I wouldn't want them to do it to any other major religion either. I like to recognize Hanukkah and other feast days. I don't go for this at all.

Chastity

I've been reading the Catechism *every day. Recently, I read about chastity and the gift of self: it states that chastity is a promise of immortality. I know chastity is a virtue and a form of self-mastery, but how is it a promise of immortality? Please help me understand.*

I think that this is closely related to our understanding of the human body, that the human body and the human soul are linked together to make a human person. You can't be a human person without both together, except in the extraordinary survival of the soul without the body from the time of a person's death to his or her resurrection on the Last Day. It's an interesting question in theology, how the person survives separated from the body. Not having been there, I cannot precisely tell you, except that all ancient Christians believed this.

The chaste use of the body according to the divine law is part of our promise of eternal life, and the promise of the resurrection of the body at the end of the ages. There's a movement in the Catholic Church called the Theology of the Body. It has been developed, first of all, by Pope John Paul II[15] and more recently by

15 *Man and Woman He Created Them: A Theology of the Body*, trans. Michael Waldstein (Boston: Pauline Books & Media, 2006).

several lay writers and other theologians, particularly Christopher West.[16] In the midst of the horror that goes on in our culture with the terrible degradation of the human body, with the outrageous abuse of human sexuality, and with the use of the human body simply as a form of entertainment—which Pope Benedict XVI speaks about in his encyclical *God Is Love*—you can see that the proper use of the body in marriage and particularly in chaste human relationships is a promise of eternal life.

Engaged couples persisting together in the absolute chastity that is required of them; priests and religious who honor their vows of chastity: these are examples of people who take a stand against the degradation of the human body by our present culture. As someone who is an old celibate and who has always worked with the poor, I want to say that it breaks my heart to see the poor so badly abused sexually, especially poor girls who only want to get married and be mothers of good families. This cannot be pleasing to our God, who made us to be His children. The proper use of the human body is part of what it means to be a child of God. That's why this command of chastity falls on everyone in his or her own way: the chastity of a good marriage, of a good courtship, of a good friendship. I would say to you, look with sadness and sorrow on how many people are severely abused because of the *un*chastity and degradation on the media.

16 E.g., *Theology of the Body Explained: A Commentary of John Paul II's* Man and Woman He Created Them, rev. ed. (Boston: Pauline Books & Media, 2007).

Church and State

The pontifical documents on social themes often speak about the necessity of involving the state government in the regulation of some issues, such as the just wage. How can the Church work with governments that approve the law in favor of abortion and who tend to segregate the Church or even oppose Her doctrine?

It's a question here of "working along with" versus "supporting." Almost all of us are deeply convinced that the Church should never explicitly express support of a particular government or political party. However, churches, including the Catholic Church, have done this very thing in the past.

Those of us who belong to democratic states would be very happy if the Church never openly approved a particular political party because, knowing politics, the Church will sooner or later get into trouble. Even so, the Church must work alongside the government. St. Augustine, in his monumental book *The City of God*, spoke explicitly about how Christians, although following the Kingdom of God and keeping at a distance the pagan state and the pagan religion, could cooperate in community efforts. According to Augustine, Christians could even support the government of the Roman emperor if it wasn't governing in a way that conflicted with the teachings of the Church. He based this on some of the sayings of St. Paul and even of Our Lord, Who said, "Render ... to Caesar the things that are Caesar, and to God the things that are God's" (Matt. 22:21; Mark 12:17; Luke 20:25).

Now, the fact is that as you support the government—not a particular party, but the government as a whole—you also try to bring it around to better, more just, more honest, more humane, more acceptable norms. The perfect example is given by our questioner: abortion. I could never vote for a political candidate who supported abortion. If my choices were all abortion supporters, I would simply have to write in an acceptable name or not vote at all. On the other hand, if you do lend some support to a party or to a government that otherwise supports abortion, you should always be in the forefront of protesting what they're doing, saying to them that what they're doing is wrong. Because you are a citizen, you do have a voice.

Now, in this country, there is a real disagreement among members of the Church and even among members of the hierarchy over how we should deal with politicians who go along with abortion. I just told you how I deal with them: I don't vote for them. Other people use smoke and mirrors to draw attention away from the issue. I don't agree with that, and I think if we got all the Catholics and all religious believers who are appalled by the idea of killing an innocent child to stick together, abortion would be ended in this country overnight.

On the Judgment Day, those people who have, out of ignorance or prejudice, supported abortion, not knowing its condemnation by the Church, may fare better than some of the believers who went along for the ride. When the Church is doing Her role properly, She tries to change society; when She's not doing Her role properly, then those in charge of the Church will be judged.

The State of Israel has recognized thousands of non-Jewish people who came to the defense of Jews under the Nazis. So also in Poland, there are several thousand such names memorialized, and hundreds of them are priests and sisters. In Auschwitz, there is a picture of a Polish priest. A Capuchin friar, Pierre Benoit, is credited with saving five thousand people. And I personally hope that Pope Pius XII will be recognized as the person who may have saved more Jewish people than any other single person. He was praised by every major Jewish organization in the world at the time of his death. I would recommend to you the superb book *The Myth of Hitler's Pope*, written by a Jewish rabbi.[17]

Sometimes there is absolutely no way you can go along with a government. Consider the Nazis. Ultimately, when their true colors came out, no one could go along with them, but early on, there were many stupid people who did. What about the United Nations? The history of the UN is not a glorious history. It has not been particularly successful, and it is a creature of the people who belong to it. It began with great enthusiasm, although among its founders was the Soviet Union, which at that time had huge concentration camps and extermination camps where people were sent to die. Nonetheless, the UN has kept its members talking. Many people get fed up with the UN, often because they don't understand it. The UN is not in itself a coherent world organization; it's a back fence over which people are able to talk. That's why the head of the UN is not called president, king, or prime minister. He is called secretary-general, which means the secretary in charge of everything. So the UN is a different kind of thing.

St. Augustine encourages us to participate as much as we can to see if we can change things.

17 David G. Dalin, *The Myth of Hitler's Pope: How Pope Pius XII Rescued Jews from the Nazis* (Washington, D.C.: Regnery, 2005). See also Fr. Groeschel's discussion under "Criticizing the Pope," below.

Confession: Why Must We Confess?

Christ dying on the Cross forgave our sins. If this is true, then why do we have to go to Confession? Did Christ's death only wipe out Original Sin, not those we commit as adults?

After our divine Savior rose from the dead, one of the first things He said to the Apostles was "If you forgive the sins of any, they are forgiven; if you retain the sins of any, they are retained" (John 20:23), thereby instituting the sacrament of Reconciliation or Confession. Almost His last words to the Apostles at the Last Supper, the night before He died, were "Do this in memory of me." Of the bread and wine He said, "This is my Body, this is my Blood." These two key sacraments of the Catholic Church, Communion and Confession, are right there on each side of the death of Christ. I think it's important, then, to know that He has told us to forgive sins.

Now, people sometimes ask why you have to confess to a priest. Well, take it from me: it isn't the priests' idea, and it hasn't exactly made life easy for them! In the old days, we heard a great many confessions. I remember on first Fridays, we were here, six of us in the big Sacred Heart Church. Confession was scheduled from 9:30 to noon, from 1:00 to 3:00, and then in the evening from 4:00 to 6:00 and 7:00 to 9:00—a very demanding schedule; but what I did discover is that it is very good for people to tell their sins to someone else. In the twelve steps of Alcoholics Anonymous, to give up alcohol or another addiction, a person has to make a confession to another person, and that's important. One of my professors, a Jewish lady from Russia, once said in class, "I very much admire the Roman Catholic Church because of Confession. It would do the Protestant a lot of good and the Jew a lot of good to confess. They wouldn't waste so much money on unnecessary psychotherapy."

Confession: Making a Good One

I know the sacrament of Confession is good for me. Please tell me what the best way is to prepare myself for making a good confession.

I've waited years for somebody to ask this question because it once was the case that Confession was very much part of the life of any good Catholic, and people rarely went more than a month without going to Confession. Many people went every week. In those days, if you were a parish priest or working in a monastery parish, you heard thousands of confessions in a single year, and people made very good confessions: they prayed, they examined their consciences, they disclosed the condition of their souls. That's what you're supposed to do: you're supposed to expose the condition of your soul to the confessor, the priest who's hearing the confession. One of the short ways of doing this is to tell your sins. People are required to tell any sin that they think was a serious or mortal sin. A mortal sin breaks your relationship with God, and to the individual, it sometimes seems that a sin did just that. Because of human weakness, however, it may not register as a mortal sin before God. Also, people should examine their smaller sins, called *venial.* Getting angry, setting a bad example, telling white lies, and one's bad inclinations: talking too much, being too pushy, not speaking up—all these things, which show different defects of character.

One of the things that is very helpful when you go to Confession is to use the proper form. For some stupid reason, they haven't lately been teaching people the proper form, and it saves a lot of time. Start this way:

> *Bless me, Father, for I have sinned. It is three weeks [or however long] since my last confession, and these are my sins.*

When somebody starts that way with me, I'm already on their side. And when you get finished telling your sins, you say:

> *And for these and all the sins I can't remember I ask pardon and absolution.*

How beautiful and simple!

The best way to prepare is to make a little meditation beforehand, to get to the church early, and sit there in the quiet. I find a tremendous help in reading the Gospels, particularly the Sermon on the Mount, the Gospel of St. Matthew, and the parables. You don't have to read them all each time you go to Confession, but read the Sermon on the Mount, a few paragraphs of it, and you'll see that Jesus means it when He says, "If you love me, keep my commandments." This puts it all in the right frame of reference.[18]

[18] Fr. Groeschel did not include this in his live answer, but before giving absolution, confessors also ask pentitents to pray an Act of Contrition, such as this: "O my God, I am heartily sorry for having offended Thee, and I detest all my sins, because I dread the loss of Heaven, and the pains of Hell; but most of all because they offend Thee, my God, Who are all good and deserving of all my love. I firmly resolve, with the help of Thy grace, to confess my sins, to do penance, and to amend my life."

Conversion and the Family's Reaction

My fiancé wants to join the Catholic Church, but he isn't sure how to tell his parents, especially his mother, who is a staunch believer in the church he used to attend. Do you have any advice on what he should do? He's very afraid that she's going to take it out on me because she doesn't agree with what Catholics believe. How can I convince him that I am prepared to face his mom and there is nothing he should be afraid of?

In my humble opinion, in something like this, the first thing that you need to do is pray, pray, pray. Pray for his mother; pray for the family; pray quietly; and, if you are a Catholic, say a Rosary or a few of them, and then gently and kindly say what you need to say. Your fiancé himself should speak to his mother, and if she gets angry, don't get angry in response. Let her express her anger, even perhaps a few times. If she is a good Christian person, she will calm down and begin to accept even what she doesn't approve of. There's a big difference between accepting something and approving of it.

If you don't pray about it and ask the gift of God for her, then expect plenty of trouble. And I also would strongly suggest praying to the Blessed Virgin. She wasn't a grandmother, but she is a mother. Our Blessed Mother loves all families and prays for eternal life for them.

The Coptic Tradition

I have met a wonderful Orthodox Coptic woman. I am Catholic, and it seems that we share all the tenets of our faiths as well as traditions. We are considering marriage, and we believe one of us should convert so that the children are raised in one faith but with exposure to the other faith. I am interested in your thoughts on a Catholic converting as well as your thoughts in general on the Coptic church.

I have met lots of Coptic people, and quite a few Ethiopian Copts working in different airports, particularly in Washington, D.C. They have always been most friendly and helpful to me.

A little background. The word *Copt* comes from the middle syllable of the Greek word for "Egyptian"; *Aegyptios*. The Coptic Orthodox church is historically an Egyptian church, though it has spread to other countries, including the United States. In the first four centuries of the Church, the churches that we today call Catholic and Orthodox were one large Church. *Catholic* in Greek means "universal," but somehow in the tides and changes of history, the Ethiopian church lost touch with everybody. They have their own vibrant life: monasticism, beautiful liturgies, and their fascinating stone churches carved out of solid rock. If you ever go to Ethiopia or Eritrea, you might see those churches. The leader of the Coptic church is also called *pope*, a word that simply means "father." In fact, in Italian, the word is *Papa*. The [then] current head of the Coptic Church was Pope Shenouda,[19] named after a very ancient Coptic saint, Shenoute the Archimandrite.[20] When Pope Shenouda first came to New York, Cardinal Cooke was the archbishop,[21] and he stayed with the cardinal in his residence.

Now, we Catholics believe that the Catholic Church is the ancient historical church founded by Christ and sent into the world to bring His message, His Word, and His sacraments. It is the Catholic Church that gives His Word to the world through the Scriptures, which were established by the bishops of the ancient, undivided Church. These bishops didn't write the Scriptures, but they decided which books go into the New Testament and which do not. So, for instance, the Gospel of Judas didn't go in.

Because we believe this about the Catholic Church, we would expect you to raise your children in the Catholic Church—but with a friendly, warm relationship with the Coptic church. And as you know, the popes of the present time, beginning with Pope John XXIII, have tried to open the doors and windows for relationships with the various Eastern churches: the Eastern Orthodox church (represented by the archbishop of Constantinople) and the Oriental Orthodox churches, the latter of which the Coptic church is a part, along with, for example, the Armenian Apostolic church and the Church of St. Thomas in India. We like to have good relations with these churches, and under certain circumstances, we Catholics can receive Communion in those churches, and they can receive Communion in ours. This is particularly true of the

19 Pope Shenouda III of Alexandria, who died on March 17, 2012.

20 St. Shenoute died ca. 465. He is not venerated in the Catholic Church.

21 Servant of God Terence Cardinal Cooke (1921–1983), archbishop of New York from 1968 until 1983.

Assyrian Church of the East, concerning which, in 2001, Pope John Paul II and Patriarch Dinkha IV made such a joint decree.[22]

Must one person or the other convert? You can only convert if you're convinced of the position of the other church. Don't convert just for convenience. It's not even desirable or necessary in this present circumstance. If you look back into very early Church history, you will see that the church that was everywhere, which was called the Catholic Church by the end of the second century, was the church that was united with the bishop of Rome. At that time, though, the authority of the bishop of Rome was not exercised as it is now with the papacy.

I want to pay tribute to Pope Benedict and his predecessors for trying particularly to open the walls and windows between the Catholic Church and the other ancient churches of the East.

22 Pontifical Council for Promoting Christian Unity, Guidelines for Admission to the Eucharist Between the Chaldean Church and the Assyrian Church of the East, EWTN, https://www.ewtn.com/catholicism/library/guidelines-for-admission-to-the-eucharist-between-the-chaldean-church-and-the-assyrian-church-of-the-east-2333.

A Course in Miracles

How do we know when something is spiritually okay? There's a program supported by Oprah Winfrey titled A Course in Miracles, *with Marianne Williamson, that I have serious questions about.*

I was there when *A Course in Miracles* was being written, by a very sincere person, Dr. Helen Schucman, who was a professor of neurological psychology at Columbia University [Vagelos] College of Physicians and Surgeons, Psychiatric Institute. Dr. Schucman had an interesting background. She was born into a nonreligious Jewish family, but when she was young, she was taken to Lourdes surreptitiously by an Irish Catholic nanny. She was so impressed by all that was going on there, and by the immense number of sick people, that she came home and asked a priest to baptize her. He could not do this without her parents' permission, so she found a freelance fundamentalist minister who would and did baptize her. She said the Rosary every day for years, continuing to say it even after she became an agnostic. You might ask why an agnostic would say the Rosary. Because it might be true. That, and the fact that she was a New Yorker. All sorts of things happen in New York: believers don't say the Rosary, and agnostics do. I'm still waiting to meet an atheist who makes the Novena to Our Lady of the Miraculous Medal. I'm convinced there is one around somewhere!

Dr. Schucman's mother had become a Christian Scientist and had read the writings of Mary Baker Eddy, the founder of Christian Science. Among its unique beliefs is what is called *philosophically acoustic idealism*. This is the idea that the material world does not exist but is rather part of our mental projection. I don't want to be unfair to Christian Science; there is a certain truth to the fact that things are not as we perceive them; they don't have an everlasting meaning. This table is here, but it's not going to be here forever. Mrs. Eddy tended to say that objects that weren't permanent, like the table, were essentially unreal. Dr. Schucman's mother would read Mrs. Eddy's writings to her every day after school for an hour.

Many years later, as a professor at Columbia, Dr. Schucman started to feel that she needed to write a book, which she did. However, she didn't make up the words, she didn't map out what she was going to write. She just knew what the sentence would be, and she wrote it out. In her case, this is not what they call "automatic writing," which is involuntary, but is rather what is called in the language of spirituality and mysticism, *sequential words*. These are words that come into a person's mind that have a certain meaning in the context. St. John of the Cross, the great mystical writer, was very suspicious of this kind of writing. I'm sure that many Catholics have read things that they felt were written this way. The book called *He and I* by Gabrielle Bossis was written this way, as was *The Poem of the Man-God* by Maria Valtorta, of which Pope [Emeritus] Benedict is very critical.

Poor Dr. Schucman did not know about this phenomenon. She approached me and told me that she was writing a book about Jesus. So, after I got up off the floor, I said, "Well, did you study theology?" She said, "No, it just comes to me." I fell down on the floor again! So I watched all this develop. Another professor, Dr. William Thetford, also a good friend of mine, was helping her, but knowing something about private revelations, I had my doubts, and in my book, *A Still Small Voice*, I wrote quite a bit about *A Course in Miracles*. I concluded that it is a false revelation. That doesn't mean that it's fraudulent. I don't for one minute think that Dr. Schucman was perpetrating a fraud. I thought that this did happen to her, but I tried to inject some realism into the situation. I was with Dr. Schucman just a couple of days before she died of cancer, and with my own ears, I heard her curse the book. She explicitly used curse words of this book. It did not bring her inner peace.

The book has many beautiful segments in it, particularly about the forgiveness of enemies, but it also has strange ideas, such as that there is no such thing as suffering. Furthermore, it is often the case that one sentence is contradicted by the next. Therefore, I would say that one should be extremely careful of this book. I'm not sure why people would read it. Some people seem to be mesmerized by it. Some people have said they thought it was the work of an evil spirit. Having had experience with the presence of evil spirits, I would tend to doubt that. I think it's better to explain it as poorly understood Catholicism mixed with poorly understood Christian Science.

What does the Catholic Christian Scientist look like? She'll look like what's in this book, and that's not a great recommendation. If anyone reading this book is involved with *A Course in Miracles*, know that, though I still have a warm spot in my heart for Drs. Schucman, Thetford, [Kenneth] Wapnick, and others involved in it, I do believe that they would have done a lot better to stay closer to the Gospels, to the New Testament, to the Bible, and to the Christian Tradition, which I think is best expressed in the Catholic Church. That's why I'm a Catholic. Given that many Evangelical Protestants are taking much greater interest in the early Church, I think they would see that *A Course in Miracles* does not square with the writings of the Fathers and Doctors of the Church.

Criticizing the Pope

I read in a magazine some serious criticisms of Pope John Paul II's being too ecumenical. These people claim to be good Catholics, but the criticism of the pope seemed very vicious. Can a good Catholic be so critical of such a great pope?

Let's look at the broad question first. Can a good Catholic criticize the pope at all? It is part of the teaching of the Catholic Church that the pope and the bishops are guided in their pastoral work by the Holy Spirit. This does not mean that they always do the work of the Holy Spirit but that the Holy Spirit does guide them. This gives rise to what is known as the *ordinary* teaching of the Church. This ordinary teaching can and does change from time to time. It's very different from the *infallible* teaching of the Church, which has been invoked only once in the last century: the proclamation of the Assumption of the Blessed Virgin Mary.[23] Catholics are obligated to believe infallible teachings. Catholics are also obliged to respect the pope and to follow his ordinary teaching, unless they have some very sound, well-thought-out theological reasons for disagreeing with him.

[23] Pope Pius XII, Apostolic Constitution *Munificentissimus Deus*: "Defining the Dogma of the Assumption" (November 1, 1950).

In this case, however, the question is about *severe* criticisms—one of them in a book, others in various newspapers—that are openly hostile to the pope, particularly to Pope John Paul II. They often attacked him for his ecumenical spirit: for his openness to Muslims, Buddhists, Hindus, Zoroastrians, and the other religions of the world; and also for his openness to the Orthodox; his statement that the Orthodox and the Catholics are like two lungs of the Church; his ecumenical spirit toward the many kinds of Protestants; and his very special concern for the Jews, which I think reflects his own experience and friendships over the years, as well as his remembrance of the Holocaust, which occurred when he was a young man in his twenties living in Kraków, Poland. Pope John Paul II is credited with helping many Jews during the Nazi occupation of Poland.

Some people are disappointed in Pope John Paul II's openness, and they don't understand how it fits with the Catholic belief that the Catholic Church is the true Church. I think one of the problems here is that any group of people, Catholics included, can get very emotionally tied to their beliefs—so emotionally tied that they don't see anything else. When it comes to discussing different religions, those of you who are mad at the pope's openness, let me ask you this: Does God call all His children? Do you believe that He seeks the salvation of all human beings? This also is one of the teachings of the Catholic Church. It is called "the universal salvific will of God." *Salvific* means "causing salvation." Our divine Savior came to be the Savior of the entire world, not simply of Catholics or Christians. He invites all to salvation. Now, suppose that people who never heard of Christ—most people who ever lived have had no contact with Christianity at all—suppose they had contact with Christianity but that it was a very negative experience. They will likely not be moved to consider Christianity for themselves. One time somebody asked Mahatma Gandhi what he thought of Christian civilization. He said that it would be a marvelous idea, but he had encountered some very *uncivilized* Christians in India. So often Christians, including Catholics, do not give an edifying account of their belief in Christ. I personally try to look at whomever I meet as a child of God. I've been struggling with that recently toward the people who made the movie *The Da Vinci Code*[24] and such books as Tom Harpur's *The Pagan Christ*[25] because they touch the deepest beliefs that I have. But I want you to know that I do pray for them.

We need to pray for each other, and we Catholics need to meet each other in a way that will be helpful to all people, not only those who believe but those who do not, including atheists.

Some atheist friends of mine tell me that atheists have a hard time in the United States. Well, so do Catholics! Join the club! I rarely see a newspaper article against atheists, but I see many that are against Catholics. When I see Catholics become severely critical of the pope or of a bishop or another religious leader for trying to relate to people of other denominations or even of other faiths, I wonder about where they stand with God. I wonder if they really think that God calls to all His children, that the Holy Spirit is working in the world to bring people closer to God. We can't bring anyone to God; we can't give them grace; we can't give them faith. No human being can give faith. Faith is a gift of God. All that we can do is be witnesses and teachers of faith. Anybody who knows anything about teaching knows that you're never going to teach

24 The movie was based on the best-selling book by Dan Brown, *The Da Vinci Code: A Novel* (New York: Doubleday, 2003).

25 New York: Walker and Company, 2005.

anyone whom you have offended. The literal and figurative wars of religion, between Catholics and Catholics, between Catholics and Protestants, between Catholics and Orthodox: none of those bring people any closer to God.

The Crucifix

How can I explain to my grandchildren why the Catholic Faith worships Jesus on the Cross as Christ crucified while other faiths do not have the corpus on the Cross?

The first thing that you should say is that we use the crucifix to remind us that Christ died for us. As St. Paul says, "Having canceled the bond which stood against us with its legal demands; this he set aside, nailing it to the cross" (Col. 2:14). Jesus Himself says, "I, when I am lifted up from the earth, will draw all men to myself" (John 12:32). The Protestant Reformers did not approve of using statues. Initially some did, but gradually the use of statues became one of the things that differentiates Protestants from Catholics. The Orthodox generally use icons or sacred painting. So the crucifix—the cross with the figure of Christ on it—became something familiar almost solely to Catholics, though some Anglicans and, perhaps in the early days, Lutherans used them as well. Nobody is saying that Christ in eternal life is still on the Cross. However, the Scriptures teach that He suffers with those in the world who suffer: "I was hungry and you gave me food, I was thirsty and you gave me drink, I was a stranger and you welcomed me, I was naked and you clothed me, I was sick and you visited me, I was in prison and you came to me" (Matt. 25:35–36). He does continue to suffer in His members.

The saints of the seventeenth century wrote about this by going back in the life of Christ to His infancy, going back to the paintings of Christ walking in the fields of Galilee, working miracles. All the biblical scenes, including the Crucifixion, are there to remind us, just as we use photographs of past events to remind us. Practically all of you have in your house a picture, either of your parents' wedding or your own wedding or some other important event: a Baptism or maybe a first Mass. That reminds you to be grateful to God for His blessings in the past. The crucifix very much reminds us to be grateful to God for the death of Christ on the Cross.

Crucifixes with the Resurrected Jesus

Could you please comment on the crucifixes without Jesus crucified on it but, instead, a Jesus who is resurrected. Is it not a hoax to take away one's attention to the sufferings of Christ, who died for us in such a painful way?

This is not a matter of dogmatic teaching. Crucifixes showing Christ, say, risen from the dead or vested as a priest give me the creeps. I don't like such crucifixes. But there's nothing theologically wrong with them; there's nothing sinful about them. The Cross has been the Christian sign since the earliest ages of the Church. Constantine made the sign of the Cross his sign, and everybody knew what the Cross meant in those days, because slaves were crucified in the Roman Empire. Christ was crucified because the Jews were an enslaved people. Had He been a Roman citizen like St. Paul, He would have been beheaded, which was not quite as painful.

There is an ancient Christian hymn, "O Crux Ave, Spes Unica," "Hail, O Cross, Our Only Hope." At about the time of St. Francis, people began to put images of Christ crucified on the Cross. St. Francis more than anyone else made the crucifix popular. Before that time, they sometimes had icons of Christ crucified but not showing Him in agony and pain. It was St. Francis and the medieval writers and artists who showed Christ in agony and pain—for example, Fra Angelico's[26] crucifixion scenes. In another painting, Christ is crowned with thorns. The image would haunt you for the rest of your life. Yet this is what Christ did for us.

So why do I dislike fancy, dressed-up Christs? Because these images mix up the Crucifixion and the Resurrection. We wouldn't even know Christ's name if He hadn't risen from the dead, but part of that great mystery of His Resurrection is His holy death. As He said, "The Son of Man must be delivered into the hands of sinful men, and be crucified" (Luke 24:7). And again, "I, when I am lifted up from the earth, will draw all men to myself" (John 12:32). The evangelist then tells us that He used these words to indicate what kind of death He was to die, a death that would bring back all the scattered children of God. So I'm a crucifix person, and if you go to a Catholic church and it doesn't have a crucifix or even a cross, take my advice: leave.

[26] Fra Giovanni Angelico (1395–1455).

Cults: Freedom for a Former Member

I spent twenty years in a cult and finally left that group and eventually became Christian. I came to understand the Christian teaching on Christ and was baptized. But it seems there is always a shadow lurking behind me. I was taught in the cult that Satan hides himself so well and deceives us so that we cannot trust our own ideas, so we have to always trust the leader. I know I am going the right way, yet, at the same time, I cannot seem to shake this mental brainwashing I have gone through for at least twenty years. My husband and I and our five children are now entering the Catholic Church in Japan, and still, I find myself haunted by the "Satan-has-deceived-you" ghost. Can I ever expect to be free? And if so, what do you recommend?

There's a word from psychology that would be helpful to give you some insight: *paranoia*, which is belief in your greatness alongside suspicion that others are taking advantage of or seriously hurting you. Cults are always paranoid.

So it seems to me that, in your case, there's a little leftover paranoid thinking. I would, first of all, realize that there is a psychological explanation for this. However, on top of that, an evil spirit may be troubling you. Therefore, I would give you the very best help that the Catholic Church can give to help you: the Holy Eucharist. Receiving Holy Communion devoutly, fervently, and with faith is going to drive this away, because the presence of Christ is going to dismiss an evil spirit. Remember, Christ is the Son of God. Evil spirits are powerless before Him.

Somebody asked me how I can be a psychologist and think there are such things as evil spirits. My answer was: "How can I be a psychologist and *not* know there are evil spirits?" In a place like New York, you sure run into signs of them, particularly in politics. So I would strongly suggest that anyone who has been in a cult and has been delivered from it by devout, careful, reverent reception of the Body and Blood of Christ in Holy Communion should allow Christ to release you from these vestiges of your former life.

The Da Vinci Code

People are disregarding the concern of Catholics about The Da Vinci Code, *saying that it is just fiction.*

Fiction can be very dangerous when its malicious intent is obvious. For example, in 1963, a fictional drama called *The Deputy* was created for the stage.[27] This was five years after Pope Pius XII's death, and this drama charged that Pius XII was cynical and uncaring about what was happening to the Jews during the Holocaust. Despite its evident flaws, prejudices, and lack of historicity, *The Deputy* laid the foundation for charges against that pope, a charge of silence that fit perfectly with the campaign to destroy Pius XII's reputation. In the past several years, there have been many books dealing with Pius XII and the Holocaust, but it is those that vilify and damn his memory that have received the most media attention.

So to those who say that *The Da Vinci Code* is only a fiction: read between the lines and see the attack on the divinity of Christ and on Catholicism. I was in Manhattan before *The Da Vinci Code* opened, and on all the buses were great big advertisements that said, "Seek the truth." You can't have it both ways. You can't tell me

[27] Rolf Hochhuth, *The Deputy*, trans. Richard and Clara Winston (Baltimore: Johns Hopkins University Press, 1964).

something is fiction and then call it "the truth." The falsehoods in *The Da Vinci Code* were revealed by almost all reviewers, and they reviewed the film very negatively. One man said that Catholics don't have to worry about this one because it's going no place. Nonetheless, large numbers of people went to see this stupid thing. It's not only stupid; it's a calumny, a lie against Christianity and especially against the Catholic Church, and it's filled with antipathy.

Now, comparing it with *The Deputy*, which besmirched the name of Pius XII, it's very likely that no one was responsible for the survival of more people than Pope Pius XII. Rabbi Dr. David Dalin, in *The Myth of Hitler's Pope*,[28] traces not only the lies against Pius XII and against the Church but also mentions the fact that Pius himself was personally very friendly to Jews as a young man. It's most likely that he attended a Passover Supper with his Jewish friends when he was a very young fellow. When this pope died, every major Jewish organization in the world, beginning with Golda Meir, the president of Israel, praised Pius XII for what he had done for the Jews during the Second World War.

So this [*The Deputy*] is a big, fat lie. In fact, Pius XII, under Nazi occupation of Rome, faced the very real threat of being kidnapped and taken to Germany. In contrast to the pope, it is well known that the United States government refused to allow a ship of eight hundred Jewish refugees to land here. They came up the coast in vain, and they finally went back to Germany where they perished. There's a book out right now called *Buried by the Times*,[29] which indicts the *New York Times* for failing to bring the news about the Holocaust—which they knew—to the American public in the 1940s.

[28] See "Church and State," above.

[29] Laurel Leff, *Buried by the Times* (New York: Cambridge University Press, 2005).

Death Experience of Fr. Groeschel[30]

I am interested in learning what actually happened to your state of consciousness while you were dead for twenty-seven minutes after the accident. As a psychologist and as a priest, you must be very interested in the subject as well. What happened to you while you were dead?

In fact, I was not dead; I did not become what is called necro. I did not begin to get cold or get rigor mortis, so I was not dead. However, I had no vital functions: I had no respiration, no heartbeat, no pulse, and no blood pressure, so the blood was just standing still in my veins. Now, it's a well-known fact that you begin to have severe brain damage after just four minutes, so during that time, they were pushing oxygen into my lungs, but it was just coming back out. The reality is actually more mysterious than even if I had died and come back. I was on ice, and I was treated by the Orlando Regional Medical Center trauma team, and I expressed my very great gratitude and esteem to them for the wonderful job that they did keeping me alive, really over a period of a couple of weeks, because I almost died three times.

30 On January 11, 2004, in Orlando, Florida, Fr. Groeschel was hit by a car, sustaining multiple serious injuries and subsequently having several brushes with death in the hospital.

Do I remember anything? Not a thing. This is partly because I was so agitated after the accident that they decided to put me under a very heavy medication. The popular term is they paralyzed me because I was moving and had broken limbs, and so for three weeks, I was out. Apparently, during those three weeks, I communicated with people. I said things with gestures because I was on a respirator, but I have no recollection of those who came to see me: many of the brothers, my relatives, and priests I work with came down to Florida to see me.

Since I was not dead, I had no afterlife experiences. But I am incredibly interested in this, and I'll tell you why. I once had a priest friend, Fr. Anthony, who lived in Dobbs Ferry, New York, where he was pastor of Our Lady of Pompeii Church. Fr. Anthony was an old peasant-type American, and he was utterly unimaginative. He had a serious heart attack in the rectory and was knocked unconscious by it. They put him into an ambulance, and while they had him wired up, he had another heart attack. When they got to the door of the hospital, he had a third. He had "coded" and was pronounced dead. They put him on the mortuary slab and the intern examining him noticed a flicker of his eye. The intern set off the alarms; they all came down and jumped up and down on his chest; and Fr. Anthony came back. So I went to see him. Now remember, this is an utterly unimaginative person. He said to me, "Listen, Benedict, I don't remember a thing. I was there in the rectory, and I woke up here three days later in the hospital. I don't remember a thing. I didn't know I had an attack. But something funny happened."

I said, "What?"

He said, "I was walking on a bridge through the fog—I can remember it—the fog all over the place." Most people see mist; Fr. Anthony saw fog. "Coming out of the fog was my good friend

Fr. Vincent. And I said, 'Hey, Vinney, what are you doing here? You're supposed to be dead.'" Fr. Vincent had been killed in a car accident a couple of years before. "And he walked up to me, and he put out his hand, and then he backed off into the fog." Now, Fr. Vincent was an Augustinian, and he always wore his Augustinian robes. So I asked him, "What was Vincent wearing?"

He answered, "He was wearing his habit, wearing his robe."

Therefore, I've got a good argument that in eternal life, those of us who belong to religious orders will be wearing a habit! There are a lot of people who think that after the resurrection the saints will not wear clothing because clothing is a thing of this world. I knew one saintly old Capuchin, Fr. Campion, who heard this, and he decided not to die because he didn't want to be any place without his habit on. He finally died at ninety-seven when he forgot why he was staying alive.

But I would say, don't worry about it too much. The other side is completely different, and you can't conceive of it. Our Savior used analogies when talking about eternal life, "Our Father's house," "the heavenly banquet," and so forth.

Interestingly, the atheists are in the same boat as we are because they say there's nothing after death, and you can't conceive of nothing. Human beings do not have a capacity to think about oblivion. It is a word, but you can't think about what it might be. When people try to, they think about it as a dreamless sleep, but if they're really atheists, that's not what they believe in; they believe in oblivion.

Depression

I find myself feeling bad about myself most of the time. I take antidepressants and have asked my confessor if I should not take them and just offer it up. He told me to take my medicine. When I look at life, I tend to see everything in a negative way. My greatest fear is committing a mortal sin; I know what I can do. So how does one stop feeling negative and get on with life and live in a more positive way?

You have a very wise confessor. He tells you to take your medication, and I would tell you the same thing. What you're describing to me—and I don't know you—is a chronic depression that probably has some physiological base to it. Often people use the phrase "chemical imbalance." That expression is not entirely inaccurate. The fact is, in some people's systems, there are small but very significant imbalances of certain chemical substances such as serotonin, which governs a person's mood. If you need medication for this, take it and be grateful to God. You live in an age when such medications have been developed and given to people. All in all, the antidepressant medications have made a very significant improvement in the quality of life of millions of people.

In the next sentence, you say, "When I look at life, I tend to see everything in a negative way." That's depression, life through "blue glasses." That's your cross; that's what you've got to struggle with. Even if you're taking your medication and keeping busy, you probably need to share your struggle with other people. Around the country, there are twelve-step groups of people who have psychological difficulties, who get together and encourage each other. You should find out if there is such a group nearby. People struggling with inner problems will *always* do better if they aren't struggling alone. I'm the world's greatest believer in twelve-step groups. Don't forget that Our Lord Jesus Christ started with a group of twelve people. There's something about the number twelve!

If you can—and this isn't always easy or possible to do—get your attention off yourself by doing things for other people. The best possible psychological medication is hands-on work for other people. St. Vincent de Paul, the world's first social worker, said, "Love the poor, and your life will be filled with sunlight and you will not be frightened at the hour of death." Perhaps in your neighborhood there's a shut-in or a poor old woman and nobody comes to see her; nobody sees how she's doing. Reach out to her and do what you can. And you will feel better.

Finally, you also say that your greatest fear is committing a mortal sin. In fact, that should not be your greatest fear. Your greatest fear should be giving up on the mercy of God. We should obviously avoid serious sin, which is a very great evil. But worse still is despair, which is giving up on the mercy of God. I would suggest that you become familiar with the writings on Divine Mercy, which were private revelations given to St. Faustina. I think it would do you a lot of good to become a disciple of Divine Mercy, so please read on through the next section.

Divine Mercy and St. Faustina

I recall one part of the Lord's message to St. Faustina: "He who has most need of My mercy has the greatest claim upon it." I find this extremely comforting when I examine my conscience. Am I right to think this way? Can you comment on the significance of these words as they pertain to Rwanda or otherwise?

St. Maria Faustina Kowalska[31] was the first saint canonized in the new millennium by Pope John Paul II. Her writings are immensely encouraging. She was a humble peasant girl who became a domestic sister, one who didn't teach but worked as a domestic in a convent[32] in Kraków, Poland. She received many private revelations of God's mercy for our time. She had these remarkable experiences of prayer and contemplation, during which she believed that Christ, showing Himself as the Mercy of God, spoke to her, gave her instructions, and made her in essence His secretary, to spread the knowledge of Divine Mercy in a decade [the 1930s] that sorely needed that knowledge.[33]

[31] Also known as Sister Faustina of the Blessed Sacrament.

[32] The Congregation of the Sisters of Our Lady of Mercy.

[33] See *Diary of Saint Maria Faustina Kowalska: Divine Mercy in My Soul*, no. 965.

St. Faustina died in 1938. This was the time of the rise of the Nazis, preparing Poland and Europe for that horrible invasion and terrible time under Hitler. And so, this humble nun, a girl very much like Bernadette, very much like the children of Fatima, received this message: that the more you have that needs to be forgiven, the more God will forgive you. It's a beautiful way of saying something we all know: that God's mercy is infinite. In the Psalms, it says, "For His mercy endures forever" (Ps. 136, NABRE). This is something very clearly known in the Jewish faith. God's mercy is infinite, and consequently, when someone needs that mercy, it is there.

Our questioner also mentions Rwanda. It's extremely interesting that we have had a powerful witness of Divine Mercy in Immaculée Ilibagiza, a young woman who survived the Rwandan genocide by hiding with several other women in a tiny bathroom for weeks. They were exhausted when they finally emerged. They couldn't stand; they could hardly breathe. Only one member of her family, a brother who was out of the country at the time, survived. Immaculée goes around giving the message of Divine Mercy. What a beautiful thing Immaculée has done. And if you have never heard her speak, I would tell you it's an experience of the mercy of God.

Believe it: Jesus is the merciful One, the Lamb of God who takes away the sins of the world.

Divorce

Please discuss divorce and the Church's thought. Many of us are divorced and remarried, well aware that we may not receive the sacraments. Yet we continue to love God, Jesus, and the Holy Spirit. We earnestly pray, attend Mass, and volunteer at our churches. We admit to our mortal sin with our minds, bodies, and souls, and we pray for cleansing. Is it hopeless for many of us?

I allowed this question because it is so poignant and so beautifully put. I think every priest knows couples in marriages that are invalid for one reason or another and wishes that he could be of help. In the United States, where there has been a decline in morality, many first marriages don't make it, and many are annullable because they're invalid marriages.

I would say to anyone in this situation: for Heaven's sake, seriously investigate whether there is some serious and good reason why your first marriage might be invalid. It didn't work, and maybe the fact that it didn't work indicates that grace was not there, even though the people sincerely entered into the marriage. It's too complicated in this space to go into all the possibilities of invalidity, and there are some marriages that are not declared invalid, which puts those people in a very difficult situation. But the fact is that two people who are living in an invalid marriage and having marital relations cannot receive the sacraments because those relations are outside the bounds of marriage. That is the Church's attempt to be objective and realistic; it is not a Church of whims and whams.

On the other hand, a couple living in such a situation could decide to refrain from sexual relations—what used to be called "living as a brother and sister." All they have to do in such a circumstance is to let their immediate family or circle of friends and family know that they're following the teachings of the Church. That's all they have to say, and then they can go to Confession and receive the other sacraments.

I think you should know that 99 percent of priests feel great compassion for people in such a circumstance. The Holy Father, when he has reiterated the Church's teaching on this issue, has not in any way presented this as an act of vengeance or punishment. It is simply the objective fact that the Church teaches that you must be married in order to have marital relations. You find very loving relationships between people who are in same-sex unions, and they can receive the sacraments as long as they let their friends and relatives know that they have taken on the responsibilities of a chaste life of abstinence. Although they are living together to support each other, they are not sexually intimate. That can also be done.

And others should, without a smirk, listen to them. That is, I think, an important thing.

The Disciples' "Doubt"

The Gospel of Matthew states that the Apostles worshipped [the risen] Jesus, but [some] doubted (28:17). I wish Matthew would have gone into a little bit more detail. What is he trying to tell the reader?

Of course, I didn't know Matthew and I wasn't there, so I can only guess. I can say this: it was beginning slowly to dawn on them that this itinerant preacher and miracle-worker was no ordinary man. Remember, they had seen Him make the water into wine at Cana, and John says of this miracle, "This, the first of His signs, Jesus did at Cana in Galilee, and manifested His glory; and His disciples believed in Him" (2:11). His glory! Now, have you ever thought about the implications of being *with* the Messiah, being *with* the Son of God? Even the Jewish people who were looking for the Messiah didn't quite expect what happened: that the Son of God, equal to the Father in all things, would come among us was quite beyond their expectations. They saw, and yet they could not comprehend. Even after Jesus had shown His glory in the Transfiguration to Peter, James, and John, "they kept the matter to themselves, questioning what the rising from the dead meant" (Mark 9:10). Even when He rose from the dead, they couldn't put it all together.

You and I, at least verbally, can deal with the idea that Jesus is the Son of God, that He is a divine Person, because we heard it all our lives. However, I think that a lot of people who think and say they believe it don't act as if they believe it. Would somebody who really believed that Jesus was the Son of God have read *The Da Vinci Code* or gone to see the movie? If we really believed that Jesus is the Son of God, wouldn't we be very fervent Christians? Whatever our denomination, wouldn't we read the Bible? If we're Catholics or Orthodox, wouldn't we attend the liturgy with great devotion and receive the Body and Blood of Christ with the greatest reverence and awe? This is a question posed by Pope Benedict: Do we approach the sacraments with reverence and awe? We might say that we don't doubt, but do we act as if we doubt? Do we act as if we really don't take it all too seriously?

Brothers and sisters, some of us are growing old; we can see the end of the road; we can see the red flashing lights up ahead. What is beyond? Jesus says, "Seek first the kingdom of God and His righteousness, and all these things will be added unto you" (see Matt. 6:33). Brothers and sisters, let's try to be the most fervent Christians we can be, the most fervent Catholics, and if you're not Catholic, then be a fervent Protestant or a fervent Orthodox. And if you're not a Christian, for Heaven's sake, pray and read the Scriptures and pray the Holy Spirit to come in, because there are no fervent lovers of God who are not in the Kingdom of God.

End-of-Life Decisions

There are continuing painful questions that people ask about a dying relative or friend. The person may be at the very end of their life and in a painful terminal situation. Is it possible for us to stop giving these very sick people water and nourishment so that they would slip away more easily?

The general teaching of theologians on this very painful question has been largely answered—namely, that you cannot take nutrition and hydration from a dying person.

Eternal Life

I need to know more about what it means to see your loved ones in eternal life. My point of reference is a sermon on man's mortality by St. Cyprian. The saint says, "We regard paradise as our country.... There a great number of our dear ones is awaiting us, and a dense crowd of parents, brothers, children, is longing for us, already assured of their own safety, and still solicitous for our salvation.... What a pleasure is there in the heavenly kingdom, without fear of death; and how lofty and perpetual a happiness with eternity of living!"[34]

The thought of everlasting life is the most powerful motive that we can have for our faith, as our divine Savior makes very clear. In the beginning of John 14, He says to the Apostles:

> "Let not your hearts be troubled; believe in God, believe also in me. In my Father's house are many rooms; if it were not so, would I have told you that I go to prepare a place for you? And when I go and prepare a place for you, I will

[34] St. Cyprian, Treatise 7, no. 26, trans. Robert Ernest Wallis, in *Ante-Nicene Fathers*, vol. 5, ed. Alexander Roberts, James Donaldson, and A. Cleveland Coxe (Buffalo, NY: Christian Literature Publishing, 1886), revised and edited for New Advent by Kevin Knight, https://www.newadvent.org/fathers/050707.htm.

> come again and will take you to myself, that where I am you also may be. And you know the way where I am going." Thomas said to him, "Lord, we do not know where you are going; how can we know the way?" Jesus said to him, "I am the way, and the truth and the life; no one comes to the Father, but by me." (vv. 1–6)

I always tell people that this is perhaps the most important statement that was ever made in the human language.

Now, in several places clearly, but in John 14 especially, Jesus promises eternal life to His followers. This is right before His Crucifixion: in less than twenty-four hours, He would be dead. I think it's extremely important for us to keep that heavenly reality before us, and yet it is mysterious, for we are all returning to the earth from which we were made. In a cemetery, the mortal remains of those dear to you have decomposed and are becoming part of the earth. Perhaps you bury someone who has been cremated and you consider their ashes, and you say, "How is this all going to come back?" It will come back by the same power that placed it here in the first place. If God can make the world once, He can make it over again; if He could make your human body and mind, He can make it over again. God doesn't have to do these things by mechanics: He doesn't plan them out. Rather, He speaks, and they are made.

As for St. Cyprian, who died in AD 202, as bishop of the ancient African city of Carthage, he had converted sometime in the second century. St. Cyprian at least would have known people who would have known people who knew the Apostles. He was a marvelous bishop and a beautiful writer who was in many ways ahead of his time. In the passage the questioner quoted, he clearly writes about this beautiful scene of eternal life where we are all greeting those who were dear to us. And remember, we will know those we loved, though we won't be related to them in quite the same way. We'll know our parents, but we won't relate to them as if we were their children because we'll all be brothers and sisters. Husbands and wives, too, will no longer be married, but they will be brothers and sisters. Otherwise, if a spouse died, the surviving spouse could not marry again because they would still be husband and wife. Some Sadducees once asked Jesus whose wife a woman would be who had seven husbands, all of whom had died. They wanted to use this case as proof that there was no immortality of the soul. Jesus ended His answer with the words "You are quite wrong" (Mark 12:27). I wouldn't like to have the Son of God say that to me.

Now, given what the Church teaches about Heaven, what do we do? I love to pray for the dead. In my room, I have a cork board, and on it I have maybe a hundred little cards with the names of people who have died. I started this after I had my accident,[35] so I could pray for the dead. I quickly realized that if I had a picture of everybody I ever knew, I'd have thousands of pictures up in my room, of people who meant something in my life and to whom I meant something in theirs. Think of all the people you've ever known who've predeceased you, whom you've loved and were friendly with; the whole lot of them, when you get there, they'll be there. It's awful to think about those who will not be there. About them you must never give up your prayers. I take St. Faustina very seriously that Christ calls to everyone in the hour of death, so I pray for everybody.

As for you, it's extremely important to keep before your mind that your goal is eternal life. If you keep that goal before you all

[35] See "Death Experience of Fr. Groeschel," above.

the time, then all the nonsense, obscenity, and abuse of human beings that is common in this dying culture of ours will not get to you. Somebody recently said to me, "Why do you keep calling this a dying culture?" It most certainly is: We have no great writers, no great poets, no Longfellow, no Tennyson, no Manly Hopkins. We have no great scientists either. Einstein died fifty years ago. We have no great theologians, no Thomas Aquinas, Bonaventure, Augustine. The only great people in our time have been two or three people who were religiously great: Mother Teresa, Pope John Paul II, and, when I was a little boy, Mahatma Gandhi, who was not a Christian but a Hindu spiritual leader of great magnitude. Probably the last great statesman in my time was Winston Churchill.

It's not a great time: we have no great architects, no great artists, no great poets. It's a slum time, during which people waste their time and energies on silly things. If Western civilization doesn't come out of this, then it will be eclipsed by other civilizations. So in the middle of all this decline, this increasingly barbaric time, it's very important to keep your eye on eternity, just as the monks such as St. Benedict did during the barbarian invasions.

Maybe this world will pick up; maybe it will come out of its deadly worldliness and silliness. But if it doesn't, keep your eyes on your heavenly homeland, which always is beckoning to us.

An Evangelical Ex-Catholic: In Danger?

My son has left the Catholic Church. He still prays to Jesus, is faithful to his wife and family, and lives a decent life. The problem is that he now attends an Evangelical church. Since he rejects the sacraments, is he in danger of losing his soul?

Let's say right off the bat that if your son was going to leave us, going to a devout Evangelical church is the next best thing, because these are churches that take the gospel and the teachings of Christ very seriously. I have many friends who are Evangelical Protestants, and we enjoy each other's company. It is often the case that when a person has moved from their spiritual home—in your son's case, the Catholic Church—it's because something went wrong. They had a bad experience; somebody set a bad example; someone failed. Maybe it was the priest. I wouldn't push your son too hard. Be patient and see where the grace of God leads. Of course, I'd love to see him return to the Catholic Church, where he receives the wonderful blessings of Holy Communion and Confession and the other sacraments. But remember, God is not limited by His own ordinances. Your son did this with goodwill, so let's trust the Lord that He knows his situation better than we do. Do pray for him, but always with great kindness.

Evil Influence

We have received many questions[36] *about the influences of Satan, or the prince of darkness. People are wondering if there are satanic influences in the world, and what should one do about it? Some are asking about how they are to know if they themselves or their dear ones have been subjected to some effects of diabolical influence and, if so, what they should do.*

A book on this subject that you might find very interesting is *An Exorcist Tells His Story* by Fr. Gabriel Amorth.[37] In fact, I wrote the preface to this book because people are intensely interested in this subject. Many people seem to be aware that someplace in their lives, or in the lives of those dear to them, there are influences toward evil that don't have a natural explanation. You can see this very easily if you look at the history of the twentieth century, during which there were people who were so bad that you're compelled to ask whether human nature can do this without help: Hitler, Lenin, Stalin, Mao Zedong. Though Lenin appears perhaps to have

[36] "We" refers to Fr. Groeschel and the show *Sunday Night Live*. This is the first of several questions in this book that are expressed as composites of many similar questions that were sent in by viewers, rather than as questions of the particular individuals.

[37] Trans. Nicoletta V. MacKenzie (San Francisco: Ignatius, 1999).

been a little bit sorry at the end, these people were responsible for oceans of blood. How did they do this?

Let's take a look at evil. On November 15, 1972, Pope Paul VI gave a very fine, comprehensive talk called "Confronting the Devil's Power."[38] In this General Audience, he reminded us, first, that Satan is mentioned throughout the Bible, including in the very first pages of the Bible, where he opens the door to Adam's sin and our troubles; and second, that Our Lord Jesus Christ often refers to Satan. In Luke 11:15, some unnamed opponents of Jesus accused Him of casting out demons by a demon. Jesus said, "If I cast out demons by Beelzebul, by whom do your sons cast them out? Therefore they shall be your judges. But if it is by the finger of God that I cast out demons, then the kingdom of God has come upon you" (Luke 11:19–20). Right there—and there are many such quotations—Our Lord very clearly appears to accept the existence of the diabolical.

St. Paul speaks often of this. In Ephesians 6:11, he tells us to put on the armor of God so that we may be able to stand against the wiles, the corruption, and the temptations of the devil. And then he says, "For we are not contending against flesh and blood, but against the principalities, against the powers, against the world rulers of this present darkness, against the spiritual hosts of wickedness in the heavenly places. Therefore take the whole armor of God, that you may be able to withstand in the evil day, and having done all, to stand" (Eph. 6:12–13).

It's perfectly obvious that St. Paul believes in devils and the power of darkness. "Principalities and powers" are names that the

[38] Pope Paul VI, "Confronting the Devil's Power," November 15, 1972, EWTN, https://www.ewtn.com/catholicism/library/confronting-the-devils-power-8986.

Jewish people gave to the various kinds of evil spirits. In his general audience, the pope points out that the devil is our fatal tempter, and he says, "We can presume that his sinister action is at work where the denial of God becomes radical, subtle and absurd; where lies become powerful and hypocritical in the face of evident truth; where love is smothered by cold, cruel selfishness; where Christ's name is attacked with conscious, rebellious hatred."

I'll be quite honest with you. I have reviewed the various books against faith, against God, and against religion being published and getting a bit of attention at the present time. I believe that atheism is sad, but it is a philosophically defensible position. There are honestly atheistic people who defend atheism with a clear mind and without a lot of emotional hatred of religion, and you can talk to them. It's a very sad and utterly unacceptable position to me, but I can see how they got there, and I respect the fact that they're looking for truth. But what passes for atheism right now fulfills very easily the pope's description of the diabolical: vicious, absurd, blasphemous, and, in particular, hostile to Christ.

I think there are a lot of people getting involved in this. They shake hands with the devil, as it were, and they don't know it. If you look at history, you will see the mysterious operations of the devil corrupting what could have been good societies: right before the Protestant Reformation; the corruption of the Crusades; the enslavement of African people; and in our day, the killing of up to sixty million innocent children. Tell me that the devil isn't behind that—sixty million innocent children whose blood cries out to God for judgment.

The pope then asks what remedy we should use against the devil's action. Even though it remains difficult to put into practice, Pope Paul says, "Everything that defends us from sin strengthens us by that very fact against our invisible enemy." He means grace.

The grace of God is a decisive defense. Innocence takes on the aspect of strength, avoiding sin. Recall the Apostle Paul's use of the soldier's armor as a symbol of the virtues that can make a Christian invulnerable (Eph. 6:13–17). The Christian must be militant; he must be vigilant and strong.

I would warn you lovingly: watch out for deliberate sin. It's a pact with the devil. That's how he enters into the lives of basically good people. When I see Catholic political leaders lending their names and their support to infanticide, I have to tell you, as someone who has studied the spiritual life and human psychology for forty years, they put themselves and probably their families in very real danger. In fact, they put the whole country in danger. The devil can wear a gray flannel suit; he can carry an attaché case. He can be quite well disguised in human life. The great Russian novelist Fyodor Dostoevsky, in *The Brothers Karamazov*, has a chapter called "An Unexpected Visitor," and this man whom you don't know, who is dressed like a gentleman, comes and visits Ivan Karamazov, and as you're reading what he says, you say, "Who is this?" Dostoevsky meant for you to ask, "Is this the devil himself?"

The Faith of Non-Christians

Although I firmly embrace my Catholic Faith, I sometimes wonder about other religions. For instance, while believers of non-Christian faiths often seem very devout, has their religion been arrived at through God's graces?

This is one of the big questions that has emerged as the world gets smaller. When we think of people who are in non-Christian religions, they're no longer off in some vague, distant place, hours or days away. They may be right on our street. I think this is a good thing, and if anyone has tried to address this, it is the popes, particularly Pope John Paul II and Pope Benedict XVI. They have been as open as humanly possible to the other world religions and have shown the respect that the practitioners and believers of those religions deserve. You and I believe absolutely that Jesus Christ is the Savior of the world and that He will come to judge the living and the dead. But that doesn't mean that God can't act through other means for love of the people who might follow other religions, particularly for people that never had any other chance to know Jesus.

How do I know how God speaks to any soul? I don't know; that's up to God. Jesus says to His contemporaries, "I tell you, many will come from east and west and sit at table with Abraham, Isaac, and Jacob in the kingdom of heaven, while the sons of the kingdom will be thrown into the outer darkness; there men will weep and gnash their teeth" (Matt. 8:11–12). He warned His fellow Jews not to take themselves so seriously, because it may be that the Gentiles will find a place in the Kingdom of God, but they do not.

The one group of people for whom I am terrified are Catholics who "know" that they have all the answers, that they've got their indulgences, that they've got it made and there's nothing to worry about. These people are in real spiritual danger because they have distorted the gospel and the teaching of Jesus Christ. I've just given you the example of our two great contemporary popes, both of whom have shown respect to the people of other world religions and have tried very hard to find the common messages that the virtue of religion gives to those different faiths. Religion is part of the virtue of justice, and since we are made in the image of God, it goes through the whole human race. It is part of justice for people to worship God; it's part of faith to worship Him the way He has prescribed.

Fanaticism

A few years ago, I had to face a problem with my husband leaving the Catholic Church to join the born-again Christians. Through the time that he spent preaching and evangelizing, he lost his job and eventually we lost our home, and this destroyed our marriage. I would like to know exactly what drives a person to this fellowship, and what do they believe in, and why do they dislike the Catholic Church so much?

I avoid saying negative things about other religious denominations. I believe in the old adage *if you can't say something good, don't say anything at all.* But I will comment on your husband's behavior. It was obviously imprudent and against the command of Sacred Scripture, which includes the fourth commandment, to honor your father and mother, which includes taking care of your family. Psychologically, it sounds as if the man fell into fanaticism, and a person can be fanatic in any number of ways. For example, when motivated by fear and anxiety, people need to embrace something. There are many people fanatic about vitamin pills, others about losing weight. People are fanatic about a lot of things, including religion. It's terribly unfortunate, because this denomination, which I don't know, seems to have at least tolerated and perhaps encouraged fanaticism. I would never question their sincerity, but I would question their prudence and even the justice of what has happened. A family has a just right for the father to be the wage earner.

Your husband came to lose his faith in the Catholic Church. I don't think it's a Christian thing to make fun of or criticize any other church. I don't think that's a virtue, and so I would pray for this poor man, and I would also pray for his co-disciples who themselves may also have suffered in such ways with their families. It is sometimes true that a family may be hurt by religious decisions. Some families are hurt because their sons or daughters join our community. We do everything possible to help them see that this is their vocation and choice, but we are never unkind and never rejecting of those who don't agree with us. That's part of the spirit of Christ and the spirit of St. Francis.

Fatherhood and Abuse

I have a friend who had a rough childhood: his father was physically abusive, and his stepfather was mentally and emotionally abusive. He has also admitted that he equates God the Father with these men because this is all he knows. He feels that God is out to get him and that he will never be able to have God the Father's love. I have brought up some passages about God and His love for us—for example, Isaiah chapter 54—and asked him to really meditate on it. I am wondering if you know of any books that deal with the issue of abuse and of difficulty relating with God the Father.

I have never seen a book like that, but I am familiar with the phenomena from the first fourteen years of my life as a priest. I was chaplain at a wonderful agency called The Children's Village in Dobbs Ferry, New York, where we had boys with emotional and delinquency problems, many of whom had had difficulties at home, particularly with parents.[39] Many of these boys didn't even know their fathers, so I was very familiar with the fact that boys in that situation had difficulty dealing with the idea of God the Father. In fact, they had difficulty calling me Father, so they

[39] Founded in 1851, The Children's Village seeks to provide assistance to "the most vulnerable children" (https://childrensvillage.org/).

called me Padre. In class, I would occasionally ask, "Do you think we should call God our Father?" Many would say no. There are a couple of ways around this. One of them is to simply call God "the Creator," a more abstract word, or to call Him "the Lord." In the Old Testament, God is rarely called Father, He is called "the Lord," *Adonai*, or He is called "Creator of all things," and that expression is perhaps much better to use. Also, a person struggling with this can be taught to have great love and devotion and trust in Jesus Christ, Who is not the Father but the Son.

Your friend should also pray to God the Holy Spirit. That might be very helpful to him when he is having spiritual difficulties or inner compulsions, or if the pieces just don't fit. Prayer to the Holy Spirit is very healing. Finally, this is one of the reasons why, in His providence, God gave us devotion to the Blessed Virgin Mary. We don't pray to Our Lady as we do to the Holy Trinity, to the Father, Son, and Holy Ghost. But we ask her to pray for us. *Holy Mary, Mother of God, pray for us sinners.* She intercedes for us with her Son, Jesus, and with the heavenly Father.

Interestingly, this kind of understanding of Mary's place in the order of things is becoming much more acceptable to Protestants, and especially Evangelical Protestants. A friend of mine, Dr. Timothy George, dean of Beeson Divinity School at Samford University in Birmingham, Alabama, has written a lengthy article, "Evangelicals and the Mother of God,"[40] in which he surveys the different titles of Mary, including "Mother of God" and "Virgin Mother." And he even discussed a title that is popular with Catholics: "Mediatrix of grace." Christ is our one Mediator with God,

[40] Timothy George, "Evangelicals and the Mother of God," *First Things* (February 2007), https://www.firstthings.com/article/2007/02/evangelicals-and-the-mother-of-god.

but Mary prays for us to have grace. Now, that's not an idea that Protestants would like at all.

I would think that, if your friend is a Catholic or Orthodox Christian, he may find it comforting and helpful to pray through the intercession of the Virgin Mary. But the first person I always pray to is Our Lord Jesus Christ. He's the center of my life, and I speak to the Heavenly Father and to the Holy Spirit with Him and then to Our Lady and to the saints because it is Our Lord Who is the Savior, the One Who takes away the sins of the world.

Forgiveness and Reconciliation

I know that we are supposed to forgive others, but my mother-in-law is constantly putting me down, hurting my feelings, and making me feel bad about myself nearly every time I am with her. Is it ever okay to end a relationship to preserve some dignity for oneself? My husband and I have tried talking to her, but she has made very little effort to change her behavior.

First I have to put on my psychologist's hat; then I'll put on my priest's hat.

This poor soul is troubled by something beyond what appears to be there. Under normal circumstances, a mother-in-law should love her daughter-in-law, and vice versa. It's not unusual that mothers-in-law and daughters-in-law have little jealousies between them. After all, the mother-in-law sees her little boy; she doesn't see the grown man when she looks at her son. Conversely, the wife doesn't remember so easily that her husband was once a little boy. The two are relating to the same person in somewhat different ways. It's marvelous if they can have a good relationship. However, if this mother-in-law behaves as you say, then there is another problem. I don't know what it is. I suspect that when she was very young, she was unloved by one or both of her parents. Most psychologists who listen to my program would probably agree with me that something is being acted out from childhood: some wound, some scar, some hurt. Maybe it would do you some good to think of your mother-in-law as a little girl looking out the window of her home with the tears running down her face and feeling bad about herself. That could easily be the case. I don't know the names of any people involved, but believe me, there's something more operating.

Now, if you and your husband have tried to talk to her, you probably tried to talk when you were annoyed, when you were angry. Why don't you do this instead? Say some very substantial prayers for the gift of peace. A great place to start would be the Rosary. I cannot more highly recommend it. When you don't know what else to do, say the Rosary. And say a good one for this dear lady who's so unhappy. Having done that, then you can take a quiet moment and say, "Could I chat with you?" Don't then say, "I think you were unhappy as a child." Rather, say, "What's wrong? I want to be kind to you, I want to get along with you, but I'm afraid of you because you seem so angry at me." Then stop talking and listen. You may have to do this a couple of times. Your mother-in-law may be defensive, and it may not work the first time or the second time. Say the Rosary a few more times but keep at it. And in return for your efforts, you might have one of the most beautiful of human experiences.

You want to know one of the most beautiful of human experiences? Well, you can think of beautiful experiences: when a mother sees her baby for the first time; when a dad comes and there's a little baby waiting for him in the maternity ward. It's a beautiful experience. When you go to the graduation of one of your kids or to their wedding. But I'll tell you one that is even more beautiful. To turn a relative from anger to love is almost a miracle. What you folks need is a "miracle," and take it from me, I know miracles happen. I'm sitting here as a medical miracle, a guy who should be dead, and I didn't even say the prayer because

I was unconscious. You folks were the ones who said the prayers. Catholics, Protestants, Orthodox, Mormons, Jehovah's Witnesses, Jews, Muslims, Hindus. Probably even a few agnostics prayed for me, and I came back "from the dead." Don't give up; pray and keep trying, and the reconciliation could be the most beautiful experience of your life.

God bless you and your family.

Forgiveness in the Face of Defiance

Should our forgiveness of another be unconditional in the same way that our love of another should be? I can see and agree that we should always forgive from the heart anyone who has offended us. But how should we handle those who refuse to repent or even acknowledge their guilt? It seems to me that it would be too premature to announce my forgiveness if the person is not even convinced of his wrongdoing.

This question is more about announcing one's forgiveness than about giving it. Different religious movements and different faiths have different teachings about forgiveness. There are some very excellent books on forgiveness, such as one co-authored by psychologist Robert D. Enright and psychiatrist Richard P. Fitzgibbons called *Helping Clients Forgive.*[41] It's necessary in many religious denominations to wait for the person to ask for forgiveness, perhaps to even make amends for them. The authors point out that in Catholicism, and Christianity in general, that is *not* the case. Christ does not say, "Forgive those who ask for your forgiveness." He says, " Love your enemies, do good to those who hate you, bless those who

41 *Helping Clients Forgive: An Empirical Guide for Resolving Anger and Restoring Hope* (Washington, D.C.: American Psychological Association, 2000).

curse you, pray for those who abuse you" (Luke 6:27–28). Now, the present question is about *announcing* forgiveness, telling the other person, "Look, you hurt me, and I've really tried to get over this and, and I'm waiting for your apology." That may not always be wise, and the person may even take it as something of an insult. Rather, to work on forgiveness inside and to pray for that person is the most important thing. Even then it's not a simple decision to let something go, to forgive, to say it's over.

Why does Christ ask us to forgive? The answer is in the Lord's Prayer: "Forgive us our trespasses as we forgive those who trespass against us." Trespasses are hurts, and so the people whom you must forgive are the people who have trespassed against you, who have hurt you. Now, what we need to think about is that forgiveness is, first of all, between them and God; then it is between us and them. I learned that from Mother Teresa. Would you believe that there were always people in the media who attacked and belittled Mother Teresa? Some of their books had offensive titles; some of those authors appeared on national and international TV. They never met her, and yet they called her "the angel from Hell." Would you believe that? I wanted to go after them and put them in their place. It meant nothing to Mother Teresa. I remember her saying to me, "Look, it is not between them and me; it is between me and God, and between them and God." That's a very good thing to keep in mind.

When we forgive, why does it hurt? Why does it take so long for us to really forgive on the inside? It is because we are giving away our right to our hurt feelings! We naturally have hurt feelings; they may be terribly hurt. The person may have done something awful to us. I know Jewish people who survived Auschwitz, and they've achieved peace. That must be an awful thing to see someone kill your relatives in cold blood. These people weren't going around telling everybody they forgive them, but they had learned to live in peace.

At some time in your life, you may be very badly hurt by a relative. Nobody can hurt you more than somebody you love. It happened to me not too long ago. Some people I cared about, and who I thought cared about me, in fact did not, or at least didn't appear to. I struggled with that for a few days. In my case, the struggle was not with anger but with what St. Augustine calls "tears that fall down inside." Then somehow the Lord gave me the grace to *let it go, to wish them the best, to realize that they didn't know what they were doing*. That's essentially Jesus' own prayer: "Father, forgive them; for they know not what they do" (Luke 23:34). Should I wait for them to ask for forgiveness? Why? It's not between me and them. It's between me and God. And between them and God.

Forgiveness of Self

Why did some of the saints seem to detest themselves when they were so in love with God and steeped in grace? For example, St. Margaret of Cortona never forgave herself for past immorality, which God had forgiven. Do you think that by grace a person can ever get over past self-hatred and become self-loving?

I have visited St. Margaret's burial site, and I've been to her home. St. Margaret, who lived in Italy during the thirteenth century, lost her mother when she was seven and had a contentious relationship with her stepmother. She became more and more rebellious and eventually ran off with a nobleman, for whom she was not a wife but a "courtesan," a mistress. Once, after she had been with this man for a decade, Margaret grew concerned when he did not return as expected from a journey, and when his dog returned alone, she followed it out into the forest, where she found the nobleman's corpse. He had almost gotten home and had died or been killed, and this brought home to Margaret how she was wasting her life on meaningless things. She became not a nun but a penitent. She joined the Third Order of St. Francis, wore the Franciscan habit, which lay members in those days did, and led a life of penitence and good works, caring for the poor, and regretting out loud the sinful life she had led.

We have people in our culture now who follow St. Margaret's former life, though not quite so dramatically. There are a couple of people in the public scene for whom I have been praying for several years that they would outdo St. Margaret of Cortona: since they outdo her in sinfulness, my prayer is that they'll outdo her in repentance. I hope that someday I can take them on EWTN and lead them in an act of contrition and repentance for all the sinful and bad examples they give, especially to young people.

So let me tell you, don't write off the possibility of penitence. Chances are, if someone like that, if some pornographer, does penance, they are going to want to do penance in bright colors. They're going to feel very penitential, and they ought to. We'll see when that comes.

The questioner also used the phrase "self-hatred" in reference to St. Margaret. In one place in the Gospel, Jesus says, "If anyone comes to me and does not hate . . . even his own life, he cannot be my disciple" (Luke 14:26). That must be balanced out with other statements; for example, where He says, "Love your neighbor as yourself" (e.g., Mark 12:31). If you hate yourself, you're going to hate your neighbor.

These ideas are expressed in a literary way; they are written in literary language. And like any text of Sacred Scripture, they must fit into the context of the whole Bible. I personally don't think that people concentrating on why they hate themselves is going to do a lot of good. It will be very self-destructive. Anybody who belongs to a twelve-step program, such as AA or NA or SA, can tell you that if you go through the rest of your life hating yourself, you're going to be back to your addiction.

So I say, write a new biography of St. Margaret of Cortona! There's lots of material about this woman. And I'll tell you something interesting about her: she had by this nobleman an illegitimate son who became a Franciscan friar and preached for many years. Margaret made her contribution. I'm glad you asked the question because there are some people who enjoy penitence to the point of self-hatred. Unfortunately, that's quite neurotic.

The Franciscan Way and Corruptions of It

I'm happily married and blessed with two beautiful daughters. I am still interested in the path that St. Francis followed. I have been looking into the secular Franciscan order, in which I have met many good Catholic people. I also meet people who seem to be absorbed in non-Christian Eastern religions or seem to veer off so much on a radical social-welfare agenda that it's difficult to see a real affection for Jesus in them. There are also other things I have heard that sound contrary to our Faith.

First, let's recognize that we're not living in a totally Christian civilization. In fact, this is not a Christian civilization at all. It is profoundly touched by Christianity, and the founders of the country were basically believing Protestants, and mostly they meant it. George Washington, like Lincoln, was obviously a religious man. His great second inaugural address is called a great sermon, and it sounds like a sermon. So let's accept that around us are people trying to do good and, as you mentioned, people completely dedicated to social welfare. In time, they may get tired; they may—I've seen it—become used up because they're not spending a little time also on their own souls. As for the Eastern religions, it does seem that often—and I've talked to people there—they're relating to an inner psychological experience of transcendence. It can be the beginning of faith, but by itself, it doesn't quite get them there.

Long before Christianity or Judaism, there were natural religions by which people were trying to find their way. St. Augustine was involved in one of these religions, Manicheism. His mother, St. Monica, prayed, and he was converted and became a great saint. So, like Augustine's mother, pray for people who are trying to do good but are going in the wrong direction.

What about atheists? What are you going to do with them? There are two kinds of atheist. There are the angry apostolic atheists, such as Richard Dawkins, who just spend their lives making stupid remarks against religion. The *New York Times*, in a bright moment, referred to them as "the village atheists" who make fun of people going to church. That was a good line from the *Times*, but there are a great many atheists who are not very happy about their atheism. These atheists do not want life to be utterly meaningless; they don't like the idea that they're going to end and disappear. I try to talk with these atheists gently. In every single Mass that I offer, I pray particularly for atheists, some who are my friends, that the Holy Spirit will come to them. One of them said to me, "How can you believe in all this?" And I said, "It was a gift. It is a gift." And he stopped dead. He didn't say anything else.

It's a gift.

Free Will

As a practicing Lutheran, my question to you concerns the role of free will in faith. I have heard you say many times that you believe that faith is a gift from God. If so, it would seem that there is nothing one can do to get it or earn it. In this vein, I have two questions: Why is it that God gives the gift of faith to some and not to others; and are there things we can do to nurture an openness to faith?

The most important thing to remember about salvation, about entrance into eternal life, is that it is absolutely and totally and completely a gift of God. It is nothing that anyone can earn; it is won for us by the precious blood of Christ, and it couldn't be won by anyone else than God Himself. No human being has a right to eternal life. Many people, when they think of eternal life, think of "the afterlife." Eternal life is much more than an afterlife, for the destiny of the saved is eternal life in union with God. Some of the Church Fathers put it in a shocking way: *God became man, that men might become God.*

Keep in mind that all supernatural grace, not just faith, is a gift. Of course, any gift must be received, but we're all so stupid, so narrow-minded, so shortsighted, the whole crowd of us—as Einstein says, "our frail and feeble minds"—that without assistance, that is, without another grace from God, we couldn't even embrace faith. Faith, then, is a gift, and you must receive it. You must unpack it. Can you open yourself to faith? Yes, in that you can ask for faith or for an increase of faith, like the Apostles, who said to Jesus, "Increase our faith" (Luke 17:5). You can also pray for another person to have the grace to accept faith. You can be a witness to faith, like the Apostles; you can tell people what it's all about. A lot of people in our world miss the whole ball. The popularity of Dan Brown's 2003 book *The Da Vinci Code* shows you in this country how many people really do not have an understanding and appreciation of the basic message of Our Lord Jesus Christ. They don't know the gospel. Anybody who liked *The Da Vinci Code* does not know the good news.

We can be witnesses to the good news, and we ourselves can grow in faith by doing the works of faith. Do you want to grow stronger in your faith? Practice your faith; live it! Stand up for it when the going gets tough. In the history of Christianity, many of the greatest Christians are those who suffered for their faith, who were endangered because of their faith. Faith is like anything else in at least one respect: it gets stronger when it is challenged. Let's pray for an increase of faith, and every day, more than once, let's pray for those who do not have faith, that God will give it to them.

Gnostic Gospels

The National Geographic Channel said there were thirty gospels, not just the four we find in the New Testament. What are we missing by not having access to these so-called Gnostic gospels, and how can we gain access to them?

The simple answer is: you're not missing very much. The word *gospel* (Old English *gōd-spell*) is a literal translation of the word *evangelium*, which the Latins borrowed from the Greeks, and which means "good news." This is, in turn, the source of our word *evangelist*, someone who brings the good news. The questioner is correct that there are four accounts of the good news found in the New Testament, and these we call "Gospels": those of Sts. Matthew, Mark, Luke, and John.

Quickly—and predictably—in the history of the early Church, there were people who asserted their own ideas, some of whom were called Gnostics, from the Greek word *gnōsis*, which means "knowledge." These people maintained that if you had a certain secret knowledge, you would survive death and go into an afterlife, and you would have things that other people did not have. This is totally contrary to Christianity. The Church teaches us that we are saved not by what we know but by the precious blood of Jesus, by our faith in Him, and by our willingness to obey His teachings, doing what He told us to do—for instance, caring for the poor. These Gnostic gospels circulated for two or three centuries. Some of them were rather bizarre —for example, the so-called Gospel of Judas. In this work, which was propagated by people who thought that the human body and human life are evil, Jesus was eager to get beyond this world in order to get rid of His body, and so He got Judas to betray Him so that He (Jesus) would be killed. Now, if that doesn't strike you as non-Christian, I'd like to know what non-Christian is! And it's perhaps the worst example of a Gnostic gospel.

There were other gospels that were ascribed to saints, such as the Gospel of Thomas, and were not necessarily infected by bizarre ideas, but neither did they bear the stamp of apostolic origin. There was no indication that they had been written by apostles or evangelists or that their authors had ever studied them. They were not considered bad books, though sometimes they have elaborate details, and one wonders whether those details are true.

You would have to be prepared to learn ancient languages—Greek, in particular—if you wanted to study them. And what would you get from studying these diverse Gnostic gospels? Confusion; a headache! The average person would get nothing out of reading them.

But more to the point: the Church Fathers who encountered Gnostic teaching did not recognize the Gnostics as Christians. Christians were (and are) those who accepted Jesus as He is revealed to us in and through the Church, the four canonical Gospels included. The word *Christian* originated in Antioch, where the disciples were first called by that name (Acts 11:26). But what were you going to call these people who subscribed to ideas that the early Church Fathers rejected? We call ourselves Christians, and from the earliest times, Christian writers called the Church *katholikos*,

"Catholic," which is a Greek word that means "universal." We call ourselves *orthodox*, another Greek term that means "[of a] correct opinion." We also engage in *orthopraxis*, or "right conduct." The implication of all this—despite all the confusion of terms in recent history because of division within Christianity—is that if you want to stick with the main body of the Church, you must believe, say, and do these certain specific things. It is because the Gnostics did not believe, say, and do these things that they were not regarded by the Fathers as Christians.

So, I would not suggest that everybody run out and buy the latest copy of the Gnostic Gospels, because all you will get is confusion.

God's Name: The Secular Banishment of It

There is a constant effort on the part of a relatively small group of people who are asking that any mention of God in any public way be eliminated. Some are now objecting to the words "In God We Trust" on our money. They have also eliminated the words "so help me God" when being sworn in. Is this simply ridiculous, or are they trying to make the United States a completely secular country? Is that what the United States was meant to be?

Obviously, the United States was not meant to be a secular state in the sense that there is no mention of God. It is ridiculous. From the first president of the United States, all presidents have been sworn in on a Bible, and practically every president has publicly acknowledged God often in life. Recent presidents have done the same thing. As the person asking the question says, we have the motto on our money, and we also have a symbol of God on the back of the one-dollar bill, the divine eye, the all-seeing eye of God.

Studies have been done by the Pew Research Center that indicate that well over 90 percent of the American people say they believe in God. Some of them do not believe that God is personal, but roughly 89 percent say that they believe in a personal God and that they must give an account of their lives and of their stewardship as human beings. This is important. So how could a tiny minority of people set the expectations of a citizenry who overwhelmingly believe in God? To me, it is an outrageous injustice. None of us think that, in civic contexts, we should use words specific to a particular doctrine. The United States was almost unanimously a Christian country up until the time of the Civil War. Since that time, large numbers of Jewish and Oriental people have immigrated to the United States, and we have made a universal acceptance of these peoples.

This rampant secularism is what I call a red herring, and it would be foolish for any politician to really go out on a limb on this one. In some countries in Europe, extreme secularism has essentially taken over. Some of them were once Catholic countries, like France, and these countries are not doing very well. I think they're showing very bad taste; they're trampling on the majority of other people. I don't want to force my religion on anybody else, and I don't want anybody forcing their irreligion on me. But when you have a lot of unbelievers, you may have to, in public, acquiesce to their desire. However, there is a strong voice of believers who make themselves heard.

God's Will and Spiritual Warfare

I have noticed that, in Catholicism, there is a focus on accepting God's will for one's life in the present moment. That sounds great, but I am confused and overwhelmed by the idea that there may be times when a person may not be experiencing God's will but could actually be under attack by Satan and his fallen angels. How can I relax and accept everything that comes my way, when it may not be of God at all? I want to accept God's will for my life, but I do not know how to decipher if it is God permitting, or ordaining, the circumstances, or if it is Satan distracting me and trying to keep me away from fulfilling God's will for my life. I am perplexed concerning the doctrine of wide-open acceptance 100 percent of the time and am in need of instruction.

This is a terribly good question, and it has often come up in the past in various ways. There are people who have had catastrophes in their life. Some of these are awful catastrophes. I know of people—I don't know them personally—who accidentally struck and killed their own children with their car. What a terrible thing! How in the world can such a thing happen? God is good; yet that's a catastrophe. I'm hoping, before I die, to write a book on catastrophe and faith, a book that I intend to call *The Tears of God*, because Jesus Himself, our divine Savior, wept in this world. He cried, and the tears of Jesus are the tears of God.

Let's begin by saying that the idea of being able to blanketly accept everything that happens to us as God's will is not what we're looking for. What we need is to be able to perceive, amid great catastrophe, at the least that God permitted it to happen. St. Augustine says, "God does not cause evil, but He causes that evil does not become the worst." That's a place to begin—that often, when terrible catastrophe happens to people, they pick up the pieces, they bravely go on, and you meet them years later, and they have overcome.

Over the years, I've trained myself that, whenever I face a catastrophe, I run for my Bible. We have the Holy Scriptures to help us, and when incredible darkness comes on me, or on those dear to me, or on people I just heard about, I think of Our Lord the night before His death:

> Taking with him Peter and the two sons of Zebedee, he began to be sorrowful and troubled. Then he said to them, "My soul is very sorrowful, even to death; remain here, and watch with me." And going a little farther he fell on his face and prayed, "My Father, if it be possible, let this cup pass from me; nevertheless, not as I will, but as thou wilt." (Matt. 26:37–39, 42)

This shows us that Christ Himself did not want the terrible, horrible suffering that was about to come upon Him, but it also shows us that He accepted it.

Don't think that Christ's suffering was the will of God. Sacred Scripture tells us why that happened: it was because of the jealousy of the high priest; because of the weakness and pragmatism of Pontius Pilate; and because of the wickedness and deceit of Judas. It says in Scripture that Satan entered into the heart of Judas Iscariot (Luke 22:3; John 13:27). If you saw Mel Gibson's film *The Passion of the Christ*, you remember that he very effectively portrays that scene. You see this little snake crawling around on the ground. Now, snakes are creatures like everybody else, but, because of the Fall of Adam (Gen. 3), they have become a symbol in Christianity and in Judaism of wickedness, though they're not wicked in themselves.

Now, in your life and in mine, something may come that will provoke us to say the same thing as Jesus: "Let this not happen." In your life, it may have already happened, even something ghastly. Ghastly things happen to good people. What do you do then? You say, "God will bring some good out of this. I am devastated, and I'd rather be dead, but God will bring good out of it." Sometimes we get to know what the good is; sometimes we don't. Sometimes a person's life is cut short, and we don't know what they would have faced if they had lived.

I speak from experience because I had a catastrophe myself.[42] Without going into the details, Fr. John was with me along with my friend Dave Burns. They went with me into the trauma room, and they both saw that I was on the edge of death several times, but they kept praying. They kept hoping. If I had not survived—and no one thought I would, especially the doctors—if they had buried me up in the little mountain glade where we friars have our own cemetery, they would have had to go on living and say, "God let it happen, and God's will is good."

I want to tell the person who asked this question, and anybody else who is wondering, that it is how we deal with the devastating things that ultimately makes us grow spiritually. It delivers us from our self-love, which in psychological language is called *narcissism*. Sometimes the only way you can mature is by a catastrophe. This

[42] See "Death Experience of Fr. Groeschel," above.

is something recognized not just by the Church: one of the secular psychologists of America, one of the great theorists in psychology, was a man named Abraham Maslow, and he spoke a lot about what he called *self-actualization*. However, in one of his books, even he took a line, it seems to me, right out of the words of Jesus: "You'll never become a mature person until you die to yourself." So when dark things happen to anybody where they are along the way, if they accept them and go on with prayer, they will rise above them. And they will be a better edition of themselves.

Grief: The Death of One's Spouse

My husband and I had been married for twenty-seven years. We loved each other deeply. He died last January, and I miss him so much. How do people survive this grief? I am happy for him, but my heart is breaking because I miss his presence so much. Am I wrong to beg God to take me home too? We were best friends and prayer partners. He was only fifty-four years old.

Out of the many questions that we were asked, I allowed this on, even though it's very personal, because, in talking to my TV audience, whom I meet around the world, I find out that many of them have deep personal hurts and sorrow, and I wanted them to hear your particular sorrow. You go so far as to say that you'd rather be gone from this world and be with your husband, and you have a very good reason: he was not only your husband; he was your friend and your prayer partner. Wouldn't it be wonderful if everybody who is married could say that about their husband or wife! You obviously enjoyed for twenty-seven years a beautiful and spiritually intimate relationship. Not too many people have ever had that experience. Now, however, you "pay the price" of being human because we're all here temporarily. However, you have the immense consolation of knowing that you will be reunited with your beloved husband and with your other beloved friends and family in the world to come.

It is eminently important to pray for them on their journey. I'm a great believer in praying for the holy souls on their journey, something that people have done since the very first century of the Church. There are tombs in Rome where it says, right on the outside of the tomb, that they are praying for the dead person. We, too, should certainly be united with the dead in prayer.

I had a wonderful old friend who was a saintly man, a spiritual writer, a publisher of an immense number of wonderful Catholic books: Frank Sheed. His beloved wife of many years, Maisie Ward, who was also a writer,[43] died two years before he did, and I said to him one day, "Frank, you must miss Maisie very much." And he said, "On the contrary, I feel closer to her now than I did before." Frank was a man of great faith and prayer. He is a canonizable saint as far as I'm concerned. He replied to my question as he did because of his prayerfulness, knowing he could be again in the presence of his beloved wife. Those of you who are in grief, try that, and you may be very surprised.

[43] Frank Sheed and Maisie Ward founded the publishing company Sheed & Ward in 1926.

Religious Habits

At times, I see men and women religious wearing habits in public. Why do they do this? Not that I mind, but are habits still relevant?

I wear a habit, and I should say that I hate being relevant. What's relevant today will surely be irrelevant tomorrow. In the specialized field of psychological anthropology, studies of religious life have been done by scholars such as Victor Turner. They observe that religious life—that of monks, nuns, friars, sisters—is a very ancient anthropological reality. Whether Buddhist, Hindu, or Christian, monks and nuns all wear a plain, identifiable garment—a habit—that marks them as set apart.

Monasticism likely began in Egypt with monks who were originally hermits. St. Anthony is the most famous of these "Desert Fathers." Early in the third century, while Christians were still being persecuted, these first Christian monks wore a simple, identifiable rope. In the fourth century, monastic communities appeared in Egypt under St. Pachomius. By the time the big orders began—the Studite monks in the East, who trace their origins to the *Rule of St. Basil,* and the Benedictine monks in the West, founded by St. Benedict, and the nuns who went along with those two groups—they all wore very plain clothing: the monks with a hood and the nuns with a veil, and that became the traditional religious habit.

Hundreds of years later, when St. Francis started his order, it never dawned on him not to wear a habit, so the members of his order wore a peasant's tunic with a rope around the waist. That's the origin of the Franciscan habit. The Dominican habit came from the white-robed monks, called canons regular.

On through the centuries, different religious habits have come into existence. Sometimes it was simply the black robe of a priest, called a cassock. Victor Turner maintains that a habit is an intrinsic part of religious life, despite the fact that many religious orders have given up the habit, which I think is a big mistake. Categorically, I say that if a religious order wants to start up again, or to get a second wind, or a second start, they must go back to wearing identifiable religious garb. It doesn't have to be the old habit; in fact, the old habits got a little exotic, especially for sisters, because they were based on French peasant garments. The sisters of our community[44] wear a Franciscan habit and a simple black veil. It marks them as religious.

Sadly, I think that the giving up of their habits by religious orders contributed significantly to the decline of religious life. Now, it was not the custom of religious-order priests in the United States to wear their habits in public. In fact, there was a time when only two religious-order priests were always found in public in their habits: one of them was me, and the other was Cardinal O'Malley, archbishop of Boston.[45]

Some people in authority have tried to tell me that I'm not supposed to do this. One day, I was wearing blacks like a priest:

[44] The Franciscan Sisters of the Renewal, founded in 1988; Fr. Groeschel helped found the Franciscan Friars of the Renewal in 1987.

[45] Cardinal Seán O'Malley is a member of the Order of Friars Minor Capuchin.

cheap pants, black clerical shirt, and a priest's collar. I was also wearing a dark-blue chief petty officer's jacket, my beret, and sandals. While I was wearing this outfit, I met Cardinal Cooke, and he said to me, "Benedict, what are you wearing?"

I said, "I hate to tell you this, but it's my black suit."

"Oh," he said, "you look awful. Where's your habit?"

I said, "Your Eminence, do you mind if I always wear my habit?"

"Not at all," he said. "Wear it all the time."

As far as I know, I may be the first person to have gotten permission as a priest to wear a habit in public. Now all our brothers and sisters wear it all the time, and several of the new orders do the same.

When you wear your habit, everybody talks to you; everybody smiles at you—that is, if there are two or three of you. But if you go alone, especially if you're young, they think you might be a kook! So I bought all the brothers and sisters a black bag for seven dollars each, and in big letters on the side, it says "Franciscans of the Renewal." Everybody knows what a Franciscan is.

There is one other thing you must do in public: you've got to smile. I tell the brothers and sisters not to wear a habit unless they wear a smile. People used to say, "Oh, the religious habit scares people away." It wasn't the habit that scared people away; it was the face! You know, Sister Mary Grouch or Father Grinch—they'd be scary in polka-dot pajamas.

Now, one of the most interesting things that I remember—and some of our audience may remember if they're old enough—is that Jewish people were always very respectful of the habit. It was proverbial among Catholic religious that the Jews will treat you best. Jews were always very respectful to priests. Always. But even more so to sisters, who could do no wrong. I remember, as a boy in grammar school, being sent down with my wagon to get the groceries for the sisters. The Jewish grocer would always have a special bag, and he'd say, "You give this to Sr. Marie, and you tell her it's from me. It's on the house." It was usually some nice meat or something similar. These days, most Jewish people are unfamiliar with the habit. If they do see a religious in a habit, they don't even know what it is, but they respond in a very friendly way. Jewish people are always talking to me in my habit. The *New York Times*, which I very seldom mention positively—I usually disagree with it deeply—and is run by a Jewish family, in the last year has had two beautiful pictures of the Sisters of Life in their full habits, apropos of nothing. One showed the sisters on roller skates. Why? Because they think it's beautiful. There must be something "genetic" that makes Jewish people like religious habits. I don't understand it, but it seems they always do.

I had a friend, Fanny Abramovitz, who sold neckties. When I was chaplain at Children's Village, I would have to go buy wholesale Christmas presents for the kids. Fanny's father was named Moses, and I would argue with him, and then they would give me a lot of stuff free. Once, after Moses had passed away, I went to buy string ties from Fanny. She was, at that time, sixty-eight years old, and she said, "Look, Father, I have this wonderful business, but I need a husband. My father is dead, I can't do all this by myself, so I want you to pray that I get a husband." The following year, I came in at Christmastime, and she looked up and said, "*You!*"

I said, "Ms. Abramovitz, I'm Fr. Benedict."

"I know who you are," she said.

I said, "What's the matter?"

"Either you ain't praying, or they ain't listening!" That only happened to me *because* I wore the habit. So that's a kind of humorous answer to your question.

Head Coverings

Men are not allowed to wear anything on their heads during the liturgy. I was wondering, how did this rule ever become established? At one time, women were required to wear something. Bishops often wear something on their head during the liturgy, but male laypeople are not allowed to, not to mention required to. I am just curious to know why.

Most people don't know this, but it's only in the last few years that the churches in Europe have been centrally heated. In the past, when you went to church, for example, in Germany in the middle of the winter, the church might be freezing cold. Everybody would wear their hats, coats, gloves, and earmuffs in church; otherwise, they'd freeze to death.

Also, the ordinary laws of courtesy apply here. A man removing his hat is often merely being polite: you are invited to dinner, you come into the host's house, and you take your hat off. You don't sit down with your hat on. At the same time, the ladies covering their heads was traditionally considered a form of modesty. They wore kerchiefs or hats in order not to distract with their long, beautiful hair. In some of the Evangelical denominations, such as the Bruderhof and among the Amish, women keep their hair covered almost all the time, following St. Paul (e.g, 1 Cor. 11:5–16). Of course, now the custom is that women generally don't cover their heads, which they did when I was a boy. It's not a hard-and-fast rule but rather a custom. If you're cold in church, you can put your hat on.

Priests or bishops, because they spend a lot of time in church, could wear the old priest's hat called a biretta. This is the square hat with the pom-pom on it. The friars never wore the biretta, which was considered too fancy for us. Instead, we would wear a skull cap. Thus, a priest could wear a head covering in church, but again, it was partially to keep him warm. The bishops' ceremonial hat, called a miter, goes way back to the hat of the Old Testament high priests. The miter is a ceremonial hat, and the bishop must wear it when he performs certain functions, such as giving a blessing. I never had to worry about it. And at this stage in my life, I'm not worried about being a bishop; I'm worried about getting to Heaven!

The Hippopotamus

Everyone wants to know the story about the hippopotamus.

If you have been watching my program over the years, you know that I keep a little statue of a hippo. There's nothing special about it, except that the hippopotamus is my logo. That's what I use to identify myself, because the hippopotamus represents the earthly part of the visible Church.

If we are Christians, we all believe, with St. Paul, that the Church is the Mystical Body of Christ; that if you are in the state of grace, you are one of the "cells," so to speak, of the Mystical Body, enlivened by the life of Christ, who is its Head. But what about the nuts and bolts that keep churchly things going? The ecclesiastical government; the people who pay to keep the roof in good repair and all those things that keep the physical plant in good condition; those who collect the money, do religious education, care for the sick and for the poor? What about all that? That's what you might call the visible part of the Church, and when it's doing well, it works completely in conjunction with the Mystical Body. However, it's not always doing very well.

I'll let you in on a secret. Somebody once asked Pope John XXIII, "How many people work in the Vatican, Your Holiness?" He answered, "About half of them." That's where I got my first insight into the hippopotamus. If you have dealt with the politics of a church—it can be any church: a small, independent, nondenominational church, which has lots of politics that sometimes leads to splits; or the politics of a big national church; or the politics of the Catholic Church, which is international. You know that, at whatever level of politics, you can get hurt. Oh yeah, you can get hurt, and people feel terrible because they think that God hurt them or that the Church hurt them. Or that they got kicked by the Mystical Body. What has actually happened is they ran into the hippopotamus, the human element in the Church.

Why did I pick a hippopotamus? I didn't want to pick a horse because horses are so noble, and this part of the Church is often not very noble. A cow is uninspiring. The visible part of the Church isn't as smart as a cat. Dogs, especially Newfoundlands and golden retrievers, are friendly. No, it must be the hippopotamus: it's so old, ugly, awkward, and mean that only God could have made it and still loved it. Remember that God made hippopotamuses. The poet and humorist Ogden Nash wrote to the hippo: "As you no doubt delight the eye / Of other hippopotami." The great poet T. S. Eliot wrote the poem "The Hippopotamus," about the Church and the hippopotamus. It's a very funny poem because, at the end, the hippo ascends to God "by all the martyr'd virgins kist /While the True Church remains below / Wrapt in the old miasmal mist."

Now, don't get me wrong. I'm a servant of the Church. I was practically born in church. I've been going to church all my life: I was an altar boy, I was a priest when I was as young as I could be, and I'm approaching fifty years in the priesthood. I love the Church, and I love the people who belong to other churches. And I'm often very well received by other Christian churches, by other denominations, and by Jews. I've had Cokes with Methodists, beer with Lutherans, sherry with Anglicans, and seltzer water with Mormons. I've been there; I've done it all. I preached one time in a synagogue on Yom Kippur—not during the service, but after it. These were wonderful times. I always try to see how God is there, in a particular place, calling His children: how He calls them, where He calls them, and what He gives them the grace to do. I have no way of judging them. I would be terrified of my own possibilities of salvation if I decided to judge people who are not Catholic, because Jesus says, "Do not judge, so that you may not be judged" (see Matt. 7:1).

I learned when I was a little boy that Christ established the Catholic Church. Over the years, I've looked at the Church's ancient history, and I believe it is true. However, I think that Catholics have done a miserable job, especially when you consider what we have—seven sacraments and the Scriptures, which we gave to the world. There is hardly anything you can do in Christianity that doesn't touch something that came from God through the Catholic Church. But we haven't done very well, have we? There was a great Catholic saint, a priest among priests, a marvelous spiritual writer, who lived at the time of the Reformation. He was made bishop of Geneva, Switzerland, but he never got there, for Geneva was the capital of the Presbyterians. It was where Calvin had been in charge. Though he never got to Geneva, he wrote a beautiful book, *Introduction to the Devout Life*, which was universally popular. The king of England, who was a Protestant, read the book. When this bishop and author died, the Protestants and people of Switzerland said that if all the Catholics were like Francis de Sales, there never would have been a Reformation.

So, if you're a Catholic, for Heaven's sake, do better! And if you're not a Catholic, investigate our history and see if it isn't true that Christ founded this Church. And if you want to be critical of us, just walk up to us and say, "Couldn't you have done a better job with what Christ gave you?"

Historical Reliability of the Catholic Faith

So many documentaries have come out on stations such as the History Channel, National Geographic, and Discovery that attempt to shed doubt on whether Jesus really existed, whether Mary was really a virgin, the authenticity of the Bible, the authenticity of the Shroud of Turin and other relics, et cetera. Just by sheer luck, I happened upon a program called Jesus: The Evidence *on a Protestant channel. It used archaeological evidence and historical references such as Josephus and Tacitus and the positive information that has come out after scientific investigation on the Shroud of Turin to bolster the teachings of the Church of Christ about Christ. For the first time in a year, I found a documentary on TV that didn't use archaeology and history to tear down Christian beliefs. Could you invest some time in these subjects or tell folks like me where we can see scientific or historical documentary programs that support our Faith rather than tear it down? It also bugs me that people airing programs like this don't provide a negative take on Buddhism, Islam, Hinduism, et cetera. They apparently respect the other faiths. Why are they attacking us?*

My guess is they're attacking us because we have some influence on their lives. Religion should be a force for public morality, but the big religion in the United States is Christianity, with Judaism right behind it, and these are the religions that get attacked right now. Islam is also being attacked as a religion because of what some of the Muslims do. No matter what the religion, some people are going to be doing inconsistent and unreligious things in its name.

They're also attacking us because we rain on their parade, and these attacks are often unwarranted and stupid. Long ago, I canceled my subscription to *National Geographic*—which I had read for years—because it had a consistent anti-Catholic slant. This was a great departure from their previous stance. But then they came out with some nonsense about the Gospel of Judas,[46] which has been panned by scholars and intellectuals of all sides. Oftentimes, the people in the front office—maybe even the people at *National Geographic*—don't even know what's coming next, because they don't keep an eye on the ones producing the programming. I don't watch television, but I see what they're airing, and people tell me it's obviously very biased against the Catholic Church.

We shouldn't be surprised, though. Jesus says, "Blessed are you when men revile you and persecute you and utter all kinds of evil against you falsely on my account. Rejoice and be glad, for your reward is great in heaven" (Matt. 5:11–12). A few years ago, a writer at the *Dallas Morning News* said several absolute calumnies, untruthful things, about me. I said to people, "I'm so happy. Because it's better than a plenary indulgence. I know now that my name is written in the book of eternal life, because they said all kinds of wicked things about me that were utterly untrue. For example, the Retreat House that I run was built on Long Island Sound. But the article said I lived in a mansion on Long Island Sound. I live in a one-car garage."

[46] Stefan Lovgren, "Lost Gospel Revealed; Says Jesus Asked Judas to Betray Him," *National Geographic*, April 6, 2006, https://www.nationalgeographic.com/science/article/lost-gospel-judas-revealed-jesus-archaeology.

About finding scientific articles that would bolster faith, the best you can do is find believing scientists of many different points of view in sciences. Probably the most respected scientist in the United States right now is Dr. Francis Collins, who put together the human genome. Dr. Collins is a devout Evangelical Protestant. You can point this reality out to people, but if they don't want to hear it, they won't listen to you. If you go to Lourdes, which was established during a time of great scientific skepticism in France, you'll find a beautiful statue of Our Lady along with an inscription that says, "For those who believe in God, no explanation is necessary. For those who do not believe in God, no explanation is possible." It's a good idea to remember that it is not the purpose of science to prove or disprove religion. Science is about material things. It has nothing to do with faith, or hope, or love, or virtue.

The scientific community must look outside itself to find moral guidance: to ethical philosophy, to theology, to revelation. That's where it will find its guidance. Recently, Dr. Martin Seligman, past president of the American Psychological Association and founder of the new "positive psychology," with which I am very impressed, said that virtue is the key to good mental health. How does he define *virtue*? Very wisely, because psychology as a science cannot define virtue, he said that virtues are core characteristics of the personality that are identified as good by the ethical philosophers and religious leaders (he moved it out of psychology); that the moral philosophers are, among others, Plato, Aristotle, and Confucius. He listed the Old and New Testaments, especially the teachings of Our Lord Jesus Christ and of St. Paul. He also listed St. Augustine, but at the top of this list was St. Thomas Aquinas, who wrote the most about virtue. The president of the American Psychological Association said this! This is like the Soviet secret police publishing the life of St. Faustina. But don't wait for them to embrace religion.

Even if the History Channel put a great big program on about how wonderful Catholicism is, I would still tell people not to watch it. Who asked them? Who cares what they think? They ought to mind their own business and try to be a little bit objective, something they are seldom accused of. And when, after twenty years, I quit my subscription to *National Geographic*, I wrote them a letter and said, "You know, why don't you lay off?" We don't need them. Why? Because faith comes from God. People who have atheistic educations and background still come to believe. St. Augustine, who had been far away from Christianity, said, "With an unheard voice, you call to me; with an unseen hand, you pushed me on."

History and Biblical Scholarship

How can a good Catholic biblical scholar keep safe from the influence of false views of history—revisionist history, for instance?

Pope Benedict, in the introductory pages of his book *Jesus of Nazareth*, has much to say about this. He discusses some of the mistakes that have been made by rationalist Scripture scholars. This is an area in which you must be very careful, and I happen to be driven to distraction by these rationalists. They give me "prickly heat," and for a very good reason. I love to read the New Testament every day, and believe me, I don't read the Gospels or the New Testament as if it were an ordinary collection of books, subject to the ideas of anyone who chooses to study it. It is the Word of God, and it is given by the providence of God through the Church, for us, to guide us in our way to salvation. It is not simply an ancient text like the Upanishads, the Hindu holy books, or other ancient books of other religions. As Cardinal Newman used to say, they called it the Word of God, but they treat it like the words of men. So I would say, study the Scriptures on your knees and always pray.

A friend of mine got a doctorate in theology with Scripture as the special emphasis—from a Catholic university. Never once did they pray in class. How sad. A few times in my life, I had the opportunity to give lectures or talks in secular universities such as

Columbia University. Before every class, I would say to the others, "I would like to say a prayer. I ask you to just pause for a moment of silence and bring yourself together in the presence of truth." Nobody ever objected to it. I didn't make them say a devotional prayer or any such thing. But they were all willing to fall silent in the presence of God. We need to have great reverence for the Scriptures.

I was acquainted with Fr. Raymond Brown[47] a distinguished, very bright Scripture scholar. Every summer, we used to teach together. I told him many years ago that his book *Jesus: God and Man*[48] is the worst book I ever read. Just to be able to read it, I had to walk around. Fr. Brown said to me, "You're talking about things that I wrote twenty years ago." So I watched his later books, especially his last book, and it was not only a book of scholarship but much more a book of faith. He had definitely moved in the right direction, and I regret that he had an untimely death.

[47] Raymond E. Brown, S.S. (1928–1998).

[48] New York: Macmillan, 1967.

Holy Communion: Exclusion of Non-Catholic Christians

I am a Christian of another faith. For years, I have noticed different churches inviting Christians of other faiths to participate in Communion, or the Lord's Supper. Recently, I attended a Catholic wedding but was not invited to go to the altar for Communion. This broke my heart. I love the Lord dearly and have devoted sixty years to His work. We are all part of His Church. Why is this forbidden to a [non-Catholic] Christian in the Catholic Church?

It's very sad. I would agree with you that it's very unfortunate. To understand this, you must first know that the legislation of the Catholic Church allows Catholics who are in the "state of grace"—which means at peace with God because they have gone to Confession if they had any serious sins—to receive Holy Communion in a Catholic Mass. Under the same conditions, we also have allowed members of the Orthodox churches to receive Communion in the Catholic Church if the Orthodox bishop does not protest that. Why? Because both Orthodox and Catholic Christians believe the same thing about Holy Communion: that the consecrated bread and wine is truly the Body and Blood of Christ. Really and substantially, it's there. Most Protestants do not believe that about the Holy Eucharist. They may receive like the questioner: devoutly and prayerfully and believing that Christ comes to them in the reception of Protestant Holy Communion. Even a person in a denomination that doesn't have Communion would call upon Christ to come into their heart—for instance, Quakers, who don't have any kind of sacraments.

I don't think a person should be offended by not being able to receive Holy Communion. If I went to an Orthodox church because I could not go to Mass in a Catholic Church, and I asked if I could receive the Eucharist in the Orthodox Church, but the Orthodox said no, I would not be offended. I would understand their point of view. Inside the Iron Curtain, Orthodox and Catholics often shared the Eucharist because of necessity. Nevertheless, the pope has said that we cannot concelebrate together until there is a reunion of the churches.

Holy Communion: Guidance for a Lutheran

Father, I'm a Lutheran and a very committed follower of Christ. When I travel, I often attend Mass on weekdays. Communion is such a wonderful blessing—surely one of the greatest of blessings—and I can hardly bear to sit orphaned in my seat while the rest of God's people are being fed. It makes tears come to my eyes. And I understand and respect your prohibitions against non-Catholics communing. My mother-in-law, a very devout Catholic, told me that I can go forward with arms crossed and receive a blessing, and since then, I have done this even at St. Patrick's Cathedral, [yet] I am hesitant about coming forward with arms crossed to receive a blessing. Is there any official guidance about this?

There's no official guidance, but it has become a widespread custom, and the friars in our community invite people who are not Catholic to come forth and receive the blessing. The fact is that, at the present time, there are some non-Catholics who can receive Communion. Members of the Orthodox churches can, if their hierarchy agrees to it, receive Communion in the Catholic Church, if they are in the state of grace. This is because they believe what Catholics believe about the Holy Eucharist, and they have the Holy Eucharist as the center of their worship, which they call the Divine Liturgy. Unfortunately, there are Catholics going to Communion in these dark days who may not believe what the Church teaches, and they may not be aware of this because they've been so poorly instructed. One of the great scandals of our time is the failure to communicate an authentic belief in the Catholic Faith to at least the last two generations of students who went to religious education, Catholic schools, or Catholic colleges.

It will all come out in the wash at the end of the ages because God alone reads the human heart, and if the person is truly a devout Christian and wants to do the will of Christ, Christ is already in their heart.

Holy Communion: Partaking under One Species

Although I am not Catholic, I have had a question that no one seems to be able to answer for me. I notice when I watch the Mass on TV and the congregation goes forward for the Eucharist, it appears they partake only of the bread. Why do they not partake of the wine also, as Jesus ate the bread and drank the wine, and I thought He told us to do so also.

This is a very good question that came up at the time of the Protestant Reformation. In the Middle Ages, because of the presence of plagues and epidemics, people stopped receiving from the cup. The theological justification was that the Body and Blood of Christ are present both in the consecrated bread (the Host) and in the consecrated wine. In addition, in our day, there are people who can't take anything that has gluten in it, so we give them Holy Communion by giving them the Precious Blood, under the appearance of wine.

A big parish is a complex thing. I offered Mass recently in a very beautiful parish in Euless, Texas, and I was utterly delighted that everybody received Holy Communion both in the holy bread and from the chalice, and it went extremely smoothly. After the

Mass, I said to the pastor that it was really done with class. It takes a lot of planning and a lot of doing, and in the Catholic Church, many people receive Communion. It is preferable to receive both the bread and wine of the Communion under those appearances, but it is not absolutely necessary.

Holy Communion: Receiving More Than Once a Day

Is it permissible to receive Holy Communion more than once a day? I seem to remember that the Eucharist should be received only once daily.

In the good old days, it was true that the only one who could receive Communion more than once a day was a priest who had to say two or three Masses. Now, we have a whole new discipline on Holy Communion. You can, for a good reason, receive Holy Communion more than once in a day. For example, suppose you go to the eight o'clock Mass every day, and on a certain day you go to that Mass but later the same day you attend a funeral Mass at which they distribute Holy Communion. You could certainly receive twice that day. Nobody could object to that. What would be objectionable is a person going to several Masses and just repeating Holy Communion each time on the same day. The Church considers that a misuse of the sacrament. But it is true, certainly, that for some good reason, a person could receive Communion more than once.

Holy Communion: Receiving Worthily

Would you resolve a dilemma about receiving Communion? My grown sons, both baptized Catholics in the military, attended Christmas Vigil Mass with my non-Catholic husband and me. The church was packed, and few refrained from receiving. My husband and sons remained seated while several in the pew ahead joined the line saying, "Want to go to Communion?" "Might as well, what the heck." My sons felt excluded, but I reminded them that they hadn't been keeping holy the Sabbath. The marine responded that it's hard for him to attend Mass on a regular basis. I now believe both would be more active in their Faith if they received Communion. We need your counsel.

You are asking four different questions. First, in order for a Catholic to receive Holy Communion, the Body and Blood of Christ, they must be in a state of friendship with God. They basically need to be turned toward God and to be following the commandment "You shall love the Lord your God with all your heart, and with all your soul, and with all your mind, and with all your strength" (Mark 12:30). That used to be called simply "the state of grace." It was a rather abstract theological idea, it might be said, to be in a good relationship with God, with Christ, by doing His will. Now, when it comes to something like observing the Lord's Day, which is one of the commandments (Deut. 5:12), there can be mitigating circumstances. Your son the marine says it's difficult for him to get to Mass every Sunday. Well, he should try, but he doesn't have to move Heaven and earth to do it. I would encourage him, if he can't get to Mass, to spend some time in prayerful reading of the Scriptures or the liturgy of the day. A beautiful monthly magazine called *Magnificat* will give him the prayers of the Mass every single day. And encourage him to try to lead as devout a life as he can in the corps.

The other son doesn't say that he's having a hard time getting to Mass. He has maybe fallen into the general lackadaisical approach to religion that is so common in American life right now. This is very unfortunate, because we're talking about realities that determine the rest of a person's existence. I once heard about a man who didn't know whether he believed in God or not. He went to church every Sunday, and somebody who knew of his doubts asked him, "Why do you go to our church every Sunday?" He answered, "Because it might be true." Even he is taking it seriously.

There are many people who would go to midnight Mass who don't get to church very often. That's unfortunate. Should they receive Communion? No, they should not, because they are lackadaisical Catholics, and there are many Catholics receiving Communion right now who should not receive it. The Holy Father [Pope Benedict XVI] has made it eminently clear, as did Pope John Paul, that political figures who support immoral laws, especially laws legalizing abortion, should not be receiving Communion. I think the statement should be strongly made against communing a politician who decides he or she wants to risk eternal salvation and who goes against the interpretation of God's commandments by the supreme authority of the Church, the pope, the successor of St. Peter, to whom Christ said, "Whatever you bind on earth shall be bound in heaven" (Matt. 16:19).

What can a person do who honestly knows that they're living beyond the laws of the Church, outside the law of God? At Mass, the friars in our community encourage those who cannot receive Communion to come up with their hands crossed on their chests, and we give them a blessing. That's an observance of the divine law. For example, suppose the person knows that they are in an invalid marriage, but they go to church every Sunday and follow their religious duties as best they can. Maybe they've applied for an annulment, but they don't have it yet. They should come up and get a blessing. Or cases like this one: people of the same sex who live together. They're not promiscuous; they're not going around advertising their situation; they're not proselytizing the relationship to the world, trying to convince everybody it is just wonderful. They feel terribly dependent on each other, and this is simply the best they think they can do right now. What should they do? They should go to Mass every Sunday, and at Holy Communion, they should come up and receive a blessing. I've known people like that, who eventually were strong enough to lead lives of sexual abstinence, and without parting company. They remained together as a support for each other, they got a two-bedroom apartment or a bigger house and, having observed the divine law imperfectly by not receiving the sacraments, they finally cooperated with the grace of God to prepare their souls to receive the sacraments.

Does this mean that I can decide that all these people who can't receive the sacraments are going to Hell? Never! I would never in my life decide that anybody is going to Hell. It's too terrible. Who am I? Our Lord said, "Judge not, that you not be judged" (Matt. 7:1). I don't know what their abilities are, what their weaknesses are, what their strengths are. I don't know how they have come to their current state. That's not for me to discern. However, I do know what the law is, the minimum observance of the law. Let them do the best they can to meet that standard.

So if one of your sons is a lackadaisical Catholic, but he's willing to get to church on Christmas Eve, let him come. Thank God that He's there.

Holy Communion: Reverence for It

I'm not sure if it's just my impression, but there seem to be different shades of respect for the Eucharist. It seems the Eucharist at Communion usually gets a reverent bow, while the Eucharist in the Tabernacle generally gets genuflection, usually with both knees bent, and adoration. Is the Eucharist at adoration more sacred than the Eucharist at Communion? Are there different degrees of sacredness?

This is a very good question, and the questioner politely avoided the worst question, which is: What about the people who show no reverence or respect to the presence of Christ in the Holy Eucharist? If they're uninformed or are unbelievers, their irreverence doesn't do any harm. Fireman called to put out a fire in a church may not have the slightest idea that we Catholics believe that Christ is truly present in the Eucharist. But a frightening disrespect is revealed when someone who should know better, including members of the clergy, show no respect for the Eucharist. To me, this is a very serious symptom.

Now, why do we have all these different customs? Customs grow around liturgy. It has long been a Catholic custom that if the Eucharist is *visible*—as it is in adoration—people go on both knees and bow. Ordinary genuflection, which is on one knee, was a sign in ancient Rome of respect to a lord or a government official and is what is appropriate outside adoration. In the Eastern church, because of the Eastern traditions, the proper sign of respect was the profound bow. Unfortunately, when people get busy, they sometimes just give a nod. And if I can be a little bit facetious, I'm waiting for the day of the sacred wink—you know, two winks if the Blessed Sacrament is exposed.

Actually, I am not amused at all by this. As some of you know, I have a great love for Eucharistic prayer and for the presence of our divine Savior in the Eucharist, where He says, "This is my body.... This is my blood." I've written or edited a lot of books on the Eucharist,[49] and I will tell you: if you want to grow spiritually, show reverence for the presence of Jesus.

I've often been struck by the awareness of the presence of Jesus on the part of African American Protestants. They will speak to you of the sweet Lord Jesus, just like He's standing there. They mean it, and I'm deeply moved. Once, after I had given a little sermon in a cemetery, a lady said to me, "Why, I thought it was the sweet Lord Jesus Himself, come down there and talking to me." She said it so sweetly, humbly, and simply that it's interesting that it came in our little chapel in the South Bronx, an area called "Fort Apache." Many African American people who weren't Catholics came into the parish, and the word went out: you go into that church on Wednesday afternoon, and the sweet Lord Jesus is in that church, and you could tell because you could feel Him there. They would go in and pray very devoutly, dear Baptists and members of the Assembly of God, praying devoutly before the Holy Eucharist.

[49] E.g., with James Monti, *In the Presence of Our Lord: The History, Theology, and Psychology of Eucharistic Devotion* (Huntington, IN: Our Sunday Visitor, 1997); *Praying in the Presence of Our Lord: Prayers for Eucharistic Adoration* (Huntington, IN: Our Sunday Visitor, 1999).

The Holy Spirit

In John 16:7 Jesus says, "I tell you the truth, it is expedient for you that I go away. For if I do not go away, the Comforter will not come unto you. But if I depart, I will send Him unto you." Why is it that the Comforter, the Holy Spirit, will not come until Jesus goes to the Father? Why couldn't the Comforter be in the world while Jesus was still in the world? Why does the Comforter need to be sent by Jesus?

The very simple answer is this: I don't have the slightest idea! God did not consult me, and I wouldn't trust anybody else who claims to have it all figured out. This is one of the mysteries of salvation, the mysteries of God.

Don't be surprised that there are mysteries. St. Paul says, "O the depth of the riches and wisdom and knowledge of God! How unsearchable are his judgments and how inscrutable his ways!" (Rom. 11:33). This is part of the mystery of salvation: that although the Holy Spirit, being God, was in many ways in the world and in the Old Testament—that's made clear beginning in the book of Genesis—Christ speaks of a very special presence of the Holy Spirit to teach the Apostles all things and to strengthen them. This is the outpouring of the Holy Spirit into the Christian world. We should be very careful not to try to dictate where the Holy Spirit should come and on whom He has come. He comes as He wills.

What we need to do is open our hearts and our lives, so that He can come to us, so that we might receive the Holy Spirit.

These are mysterious things that are part of the life of God, part of the mystery of the Holy Trinity, and although people may speculate and give reasons that sound good about why Christ had to send the Holy Spirit, what I would rather do is wait till I get there. This is one of the several questions I'm going to be asking.

The riches, the wisdom, and knowledge of God!

The Human Body Glorified

If our bodies are to be glorified at the resurrection of the dead, does this mean that Heaven is not just a spiritual world but an actual physical place where we can function as we have on earth—for example, play baseball? I read that when our bodies are glorified, we'll be able to pass through matter, but will we be able to touch and hold things, as we do here on earth whenever we want to?

The key word here is *mystery*; we are dealing with entirely mysterious things. As Pope [Emeritus] Benedict points out in his encyclical *Spe Salvi*, "Saved in Hope," we have no adequate understanding of what eternal life is like because we don't have a concept of eternity. In fact, the pope says that if you just sit down and think about an eternal succession of days, it doesn't sound very attractive. We don't understand what the physical world will be like then, but it has been a traditional Christian teaching, based particularly on the writings of St. Paul and on the Gospels, that somehow or other, at the end of the ages, you get your body back.

What about people who burned to death? What about people who died in the sea? There is no difference for anyone: somehow or other, God gives you a corporeal body. Whether it looks much like what we have now I don't know. Personally, I hope it's different. I wouldn't like to go back to having a broken arm! St. Paul says, "What no eye has seen, nor ear heard, nor the heart of man conceived, what God has prepared for those who love Him" (1 Cor. 2:9). We can't really even think about it!

Furthermore, we're not even too sure what we mean by "material substance." Einstein worked on that for a long time. Next to me is a table. Try as I might, my hand can't pass through the table, but perhaps that won't be the case in eternity. We just don't know what all these things really are. We don't have adequate conceptualizations of them. So, I say wait and see; be surprised, because we do pass into a far better world, where there is neither mourning, nor weeping, nor crying anymore.

If you're interested, read the last three chapters of the book of Revelation, which are marvelous, mysterious chapters of what eternal life is like.

Humility: Genuine

What is the line between true humility and being a doormat and an emotional punching bag for people around me? I'm very confused whether I should accept abuse from others or whether I should humbly accept it.

First off, we are not talking about false humility, where a person pretends to be humble, but rather about a person accepting other people's shortcomings and/or their abuse and smiling through it. That can be a real act of humility, and perhaps most of the people reading this book have done just that in a given situation. Somebody's having a bad day or has a bad temper—somebody in your family, somebody you know. You calmly take it with both humility and wisdom because you know it's going to pass. It's not worth getting upset about. But as our questioner points out, you can become a doormat or a punching bag, and that's bad. There is a fairly large number of people in the world who don't realize that their personalities are masochistic. This is probably because of things they suffered in childhood, and it tends to invite other people to abuse or to belittle them.

There are also many aggressive people in the world. They are looking for punching bags, and so masochistic people who come along are natural punching bags. If you see the latter in yourself, true humility for you is getting over that and quietly and calmly saying to those who would be abusive, "Is there something wrong?

Aren't you feeling well today?" Do not ask, "Did I do something wrong?" because they'll have a list. Never use the phrase, "I can stand anything but that," because the sadist will then do just that. Instead, as in tennis, hit the ball back over the net. If you approach such people this way, I think you may find that they keep quiet, especially if you do it in a very mature, kindly way.

When I say "sadist" and "masochist," I'm referring to potentially very serious psychological problems, where some people, masochists, physically attract abuse and others, sadists, physically give abuse. But there is a very subtle, neurotic form of masochism that enjoys being kicked around; and there is a very subtle sadism, a polite, elegant way of taking your aggravation out on people and hurting them. There are even some people who are *both*. That's a really serious problem. Half the time, they're inviting punishment, and the other half, they're giving it out. That's called "sadomasochism," and it's really confused.

It's best to accept criticism, which you can use, especially if it's given positively, but it is not wise simply to accept the peak aggravation and annoyance of others. I happen to be somebody who likes to do things quickly. I tend to be rash. That makes me appear impatient, and in fact, I am impatient. The brothers and the others who work with me at our retreat house know just how to handle me. They're very nice, they're very sweet, and immediately I begin to feel guilty; I begin to feel like a jerk. It's a very helpful tool, to somebody who is intense, who does things quickly, who likes to get the job done, to be quiet, dispassionate, and gentle. This very morning, I was late to the studio because, though Brother Paolo duly arrived on time, nobody told me. I was a bit sharp. The brother to whom I was sharp takes marvelous care of me in my infirmity. He just smiled. When the day is over and I make my examination of conscience and my act of contrition, he'll get an extra little prayer, and so will brother Paolo.

Illegal Immigration

I try to do what is right. Please explain to me the true Christian response to those who enter the United States unlawfully and those who wait and follow the legal procedure. Is there a way that everyone—illegal or legal, undocumented or documented, foreigner or native—can be treated fairly and act as an adult Christian toward others and toward himself, including his country?

It is extremely important to remember that, legal or illegal, all these people are human beings. As St. Thomas Aquinas says so clearly, the earth belongs to humanity, it doesn't belong to a particular nation, and so the natural law oftentimes takes precedence over national law.

Why do the people come illegally? Most come because they're desperate for food and for a way to support their families. Thus, the laws against immigration are not moral laws, they're not part of the Ten Commandments. They are something like traffic laws; they keep things orderly and safe. It's not morally different whether you go twenty-five or thirty miles an hour; that's a civil law. I would say that immigration laws basically have that purpose. But in the United States, there are two things weighing against those laws. First, we have desperately poor people in Latin America, especially in Mexico, who desperately need work. When people are desperately poor, they're not even obliged sometimes by the moral law. Moral theologians have always said that the starving person can steal a loaf of bread because the bread ultimately belongs to God. That's classic moral theology. The popes have reiterated repeatedly that human ownership is not absolute, that the things of the world are *given* to everyone. Popes Leo XIII, Pius XII, John XXIII, and John Paul II all taught social responsibility and that societies exist for the benefit of all the citizens because God made the world for everybody. So keep that in mind, that immigration laws do not have the force of laws like "You shall not commit adultery; you shall not steal."

Also, it's extremely important to know that these people are here with the connivance of the government. There are eleven million illegal workers in the United States.[50] If they do come, they must have a green card, so they buy a phony green card from a counterfeiter for a hundred dollars. It costs the counterfeiter about fifty cents to make it, and it has a made-up number on it. When he earns his first week's wages, the employer remits the withholding, including Social Security, along with the green-card number. Months later, out of the computer in Washington will come a letter telling them that they sent in the wrong number and to please send in the right number. They send in another made-up number, and they never hear anything about it again.

Now, perhaps the government has changed this practice, but I have talked to undocumented people who never heard again from the government, and all undocumented people are aware of this. That is what I mean by the connivance of the federal government. Because of that connivance, we have a gigantic problem: eleven million people—that's the population of a small country—cannot

[50] As of the airing of this program, circa 2007.

suddenly be moved out. Moreover, the government has them here because they're necessary for our agriculture and many of the other services that they provide. It is my understanding that, in several places in the United States, undocumented Latino workers have had day-long work stoppages, and for the duration nothing went on. You heard no grass cutters or weed whackers; on the farms, no plows were operating. I have talked to important people in significant parts of agriculture, particularly in the far West, including vintners and farmers who grow all kinds of produce, who have told me that almost all their workers are undocumented. Also, many political leaders, including senators and congressmen, have said that agriculture will stop in their state if everyone is put out.

How did this situation occur? For years, workers had the ability to apply for a work permit. It wasn't a green card; it didn't get them here permanently; but they could work for months and months with the work permit, go back home, reapply, and get another work permit. This was stopped because of pressure from labor unions, who should be ashamed of themselves because people who belong to labor unions are not going to work on the farms. It's backbreaking work for relatively little pay.

If our country depends so significantly on these workers, they have a right to be treated fairly and with understanding, and they are not. There are four sins in the Bible that "cry to heaven for vengeance": murder (Gen. 4:10), sodomy (Gen. 18:20–21), oppression of the poor (Exod. 2:23), and depriving workers of their wages (James 5:4). All these eleven million people pay Social Security, and they will never collect a single penny. It's a severe injustice. I figured it out mathematically that they are paying at least two and a half billion dollars a year into the shaky Social Security system. So if you're on Social Security, you should know that some of your income is earned by people who will never benefit from it themselves. I am deeply distressed that some politicians who pride themselves on being pro-life are also outstanding in their coolness toward the treatment of undocumented workers.

Popes Benedict XVI and John Paul II have spoken clearly about the treatment of the poor. Economically, we have been an extremely powerful nation, and any student of history will tell you that the United States has, for decades, drained the natural resources of its poorer and weaker neighbors, and because of that, we're immensely unpopular. People ask me how Fidel Castro stayed in power so long with an unjust tyrannical government. Because he was hostile to the United States, that's how he got started. The United States abused and misused Cuba, and it has done the same thing with other Latin American nations. Don't be surprised by this because a big nation will do this unless its leaders are very morally aware of their responsibility. Many people south of the Mexican border are very poor, and that is something to be concerned about. The United States is stained by several terrible injustices in its history: the treatment of Africans brought here under slavery; the treatment of their children; and racial segregation, which lasted way up until the 1970s and was broken by a charismatic Protestant minister, Martin Luther King, helped by many others.

We also have another sin that cries to Heaven for vengeance, and that is a willful murder of almost sixty million defenseless unborn children. We're now going to add another one: depriving the poor of their wages. Think about it: practically 90 percent of the people reading this book were born in this country because their ancestors faced a dangerous sea voyage to come to America to give their children a chance. That's very important.

This is the position of the Catholic Church. And I think you could make a very good case that, even more than that, it is the position of the Old and New Testaments.

The Image of God

How do we define men being made in God's image? We are physical beings with souls, but God is pure spirit. We think as creatures think, not as the Creator thinks; we live in time, whereas God is outside of time. If we do not resemble God in body or mind or dimension, why do we say we are made in God's image? Is it pure conceit?

No, I wouldn't say it's pure conceit; but your question is an excellent one, and it shows a good deal of thought.

What you say is true: we are not pure spirit; we think as rational creatures think. We come to conclusions, thinking slowly. Unlike the angels, we don't perceive things by an instant intuition. We live in time, and God is not in time. In what sense, then, are we made in God's image? Now, this is an abstract question that requires an abstract answer, so hang on. We are made in God's image because we exist; He has shared with us existence. Now, that may be a hard thing to comprehend, but think of nonexistence. Try to think of nothing. Think of what's beyond all the stars, just nothing waiting to become something. You can't do it because that's not what we are. We are already something, we have existence in time, something given to us by God, which is very beautiful.

Also, God's image is found in us because we can think and reason. Admittedly, our thinking and reasoning is far inferior to

God's, but we can do it. If you watch animals, particularly domesticated animals such as golden retrievers and Newfoundlands, they sometimes seem almost human, because they know how to relate to us and how to get us to be very kind to them. But they don't think abstractly, as we do. They can't consider their own natures and stand back and say, "It's me, Fido, who's doing this thinking." They don't have that reflective knowledge of self; they live in an intense present. You might say that they're existential. They do think, but not rationally.

They also have various instincts, some of which are being studied right now—a very fascinating area of research. We thought that animals were either solitary or just had a sort of herd mentality, in either case with a pecking order or just different ways of doing things. But these are not planned out; they come from impulses within them. Human beings also do a lot of things according to impulses, but we can, in our better moments, rationally go beyond our mere impulses, and in that, we are somewhat like God. It is for this reason that we have an eternal destiny.

The *In Paradisum* Prayer

I'm a lifelong Protestant, feeling a pull to the Catholic Church, and the information I get from the [EWTN] Network in general, and from Fr. Groeschel in particular, is very helpful. Months ago, Father spoke of his early years in the Church; he told of the nuns who taught him to pray for the dead and to pray for the bereaved, the ones left behind to grieve the dead. The prayer he recited reduced me to tears, and I should have written it down. Now, when I have many friends losing loved ones, for whom I would like to pray with more eloquence, I cannot recall that prayer. Is there a chance I could get that prayer from you?

You are referring to a very beautiful prayer called in Latin *In Paradisum*. It is the last thing in the Requiem Mass of Gabriel Fauré, and he does it very beautifully:

> *May the angels lead you into paradise. May the martyrs come and welcome you on your way, and bring you to the holy city, Jerusalem. May the choir of angels welcome you. And with Lazarus who was once so poor, may you have life everlasting. Amen.*

Many priests say that prayer at the end of the funeral rite. In the final prayers before they go to the cemetery, they will say the *In Paradisum* in English.

Jesus' Divinity

As you know, there has been a great attack on the divinity of Jesus Christ over the past several decades. One of the things I often hear is Jesus Christ spoken of as a human. No mere human being could save us; only God can save us. I'm more and more convinced that the era of calling Jesus a human being is at the root of so many problems that we are facing in the Church today. I like what St. Cyril of Alexandria helped us to see. Namely, Jesus Christ is God in flesh. There seems to be a much better way to speak of the mystery of the Incarnation

I couldn't agree with you more. St. Cyril, a Doctor of the Church, was the archbishop of Alexandria, who presided over the Council of Ephesus in 431. Nestorius, the archbishop of Constantinople, had forbidden people to call Mary "the mother of God," saying instead that Mary was the "mother of Jesus of Nazareth" but is not the mother of the Eternal Word. The net effect of Nestorius's distinction is that you end up with two persons: Jesus the human being glued, as it were, to God. This is a kind of dualism, and it plunged the Church into confrontation at the Council of Ephesus, with St. Cyril on one side and Nestorius on the other. Though called by Nestorius himself, the council found against him and issued a decree to this effect: that at a certain moment in time, the Second Person of the blessed Trinity, the eternal Word of

God, equal to the Father in all things, took upon Himself a true human body and a true human soul in the womb of the glorious Virgin Mary. So, calling Jesus a human being or a human person is inaccurate: Jesus is a divine Person who has taken upon Himself humanity. He certainly has a human body and soul and so is in every respect human (Heb. 2:17), but as to His personhood, He is divine.

Let me illustrate this to you. Years ago, I was down in West Point, Alabama. I was invited to a Baptist church to speak on the spiritual life. I, of course, loved to talk to them: they're well informed, they love the Scriptures, and, like St. Francis and the Franciscans, they like simplicity. As an aside, I remember years ago bringing a Baptist minister to the chapel of our monastery. Once inside, he looked at me and said, "Why, it looks absolutely Baptist!"—because the monastery was very plain.

The Baptist church was large. I think there were six hundred or seven hundred laypeople present, and, in the front rows, there were quite a few ministers, maybe twenty or thirty of them. Even though it wasn't the topic of my talk, I knew the question would come: "Why do you Catholics call Mary 'the Mother of God'?" When it came, I said, "Well, is Jesus Christ divine?"

They said, "Yes."

"Is He human?" I asked.

"Yes."

"Is Jesus a divine person?"

"Yes."

"Is He a human person?"

The ministers all said, "No," but some of the laypeople said, "Yes."

I said, "Well, if He is a divine person but isn't God the Father, and not God the Holy Spirit, but God the Son, the second Person of the Most Holy Trinity, if He was born to human flesh, isn't this what Christmas is about?"

I continued: "Can you say that God suffered?

"Yes."

"Can you say that God was crucified?"

"Yes."

"Can you say that God died? What I mean is, did God experience human death?"

"Yes."

"So God was born."

"Yes."

"Then God had a mother."

"Yes."

"So, Mary is the mother of God," I said, and the light suddenly went on for the people present, and the minister rather solemnly said, "Yeah"—because the minister didn't want to be a Nestorian heretic.

Protestants don't like the title "Mother of God," but it goes back all the way to the very earliest period of the Church. In Greek, it's *Theotokos*, which means "God-bearer," and it was proclaimed an essential teaching of the Church at the Council of Ephesus by St. Cyril, the archbishop of Alexandria. Now, I'm perfectly happy to let my good Protestant friends not *call* Mary the Mother of God, but they have to know that she in fact *is*, or they're going to be Nestorian.

On the other hand, there are some people who really annoy me, having put out smart-aleck books—for instance, *The Pagan Christ* by Tom Harpur and *The Jesus Dynasty* by James Tabor.[51] These, along with several other flaky writings that you can find in the big book

[51] New York: Simon & Schuster, 2006.

shops, following in the footsteps of Dan Brown's *Da Vinci Code*,[52] all claim that Christ is a creation of the Catholic Church. But is what they point their fingers at really the Catholic Church? The Church of the bishops of the apostolic succession? The Catholic Church has handed on divine authority, received from Jesus Himself (Matt. 16:17–19), from one generation to the next, beginning with the Apostles. These bishops of the apostolic Church, which is called, as I explained to you, Catholic, or universal, have guided the faithful, clinging to the Scriptures and developing Tradition, which isn't in the Scriptures but is the authoritative Christian interpretation of the Scriptures. For example, it's from Tradition, not the Scriptures, that we get "Jesus, son of God, equal to the Father in all things"—that is, based on the Scriptures interpreted traditionally.

[52] New York: Doubleday, 2003.

Jesus: Resurrected and Unrecognized

In Scripture, after the Resurrection, Our Lord appears to several people, yet they do not recognize Him at the time that they are seeing Him. They do not realize it is He until after He breaks the bread at their table; then He disappears. Could you explain this?

I wasn't there, and I get very annoyed at people who were not there and yet "know" what happened. This is an utterly mysterious event. A Person who was dead, body ripped apart, crucified, and buried for three days, yet who rises from the dead. This is utterly unprecedented.

What is He like now? We don't know. I've never seen anybody rise from the dead. At least on the road to Emmaus (Luke 24:13–35), the passage that the questioner is referring to, the disciples do not seem to know Him. It says, "their eyes were kept from recognizing Him" (v. 16). It was in the late part of the day, and they only knew Him "in the breaking of the bread" (v. 35). Earlier that same day, Mary Magdalene, who was very upset, didn't recognize Him. She thought He was the gardener. The last person she ever expected to meet was Jesus.

At other times, the Apostles did recognize Him immediately. While fishing, apparently in vain, they once saw Him standing on the shore of the Sea of Galilee. They only suspected it was

Jesus when He told them to put down their nets on the right side of the boat and they immediately caught a whole lot of fish. John said, "It is the Lord!" and Peter jumped in and swam to shore (John 21:4–8). I walked along that shoreline early in the morning one day, right by the ruins of Capernaum, imagining what that must have been like that day. It was a very precious moment. But I wasn't there, and neither was anybody else who's alive right now, so none of us really know what it was like to see and yet not recognize Jesus. As a psychologist, not a Scripture scholar, I guess that if you were not expecting at all to see someone and you saw him in an impossible situation, you might not recognize him. Now, hardly ever do we see someone who is totally outside of our range of expectations, but it could happen, and for a few minutes, you might not realize who it was. Perhaps that's what this Scripture passage is talking about. But maybe it's a somewhat supernatural phenomenon, particularly with the disciples of Emmaus, because it says, "Their eyes were kept." I don't know what that means, because, to my knowledge, my eyes were never held, and nobody else around seems to me to know what it means either. As for the people who do "know" what it means, I don't listen to them.

I remember one of my favorite stories about my old Jewish neighbor Mrs. Nilbaum and her smart-aleck son, Alex. One day, while he was in junior college, he came to her and said, "Mama, he had it all wrong. When Moses came through the Red Sea, it was a low tide." She responded, "You were there?" He said, "I wasn't there, and nobody else around was there." When we encounter these events in the Scriptures, it might be a very appropriate moment for people to shut up and sit there in the mystery of Christ. Too many people tell me too many things about Christ, especially after His death, and I'm not inclined to take them too seriously.

Jesus' Healings: Why Did He Try to Keep Them Quiet?

I have been reading the Gospels during Lent and have noticed repeatedly that Jesus keeps telling those individuals whom He cures not to tell anyone. An example is from Mark 7:31–37, where He heals the deaf man. Why does He keep saying this? Is He trying to teach us to be humble and not self-promoters?

Well, it's very difficult when you try to read the mind of Jesus. Why does He do this, that, or the other thing? Anybody's answer to those questions is a speculation. It would seem, though, that He was trying to control the crowds. Wherever He went, there were surging crowds waiting to see Him because they wanted healing or other miraculous things. My suspicion is that He told him not to tell anybody so He would get a little bit of peace and be able to move on, but that's just a guess. I can see our divine Savior saying, "Now listen, please don't tell anybody. I've got to get through here very soon. I've got an appointment in Jerusalem." It's a bit of a funny answer, but maybe it is the reason. But speculating about why Jesus did or said things that we don't understand is potentially dangerous business.

Job Situation: Hostile Boss

I suspect my boss is anti-Christian [because she] has made it known that she wants religious items such as crosses removed from our offices. I still have mine up, and I'm not sure how I will respond if I am directly told to remove it. I really do feel a strong sense of comfort having it there. If I remove it, I will feel a great sense of loss. It seems America isn't as free as it used to be. How do you think I should respond? Should I keep it there or place it behind something so it can't be seen?

The first thing you want to take into consideration, believe it or not, is *how are you going to help your boss?* Your boss is a person with an immortal soul, even if she's anti-Christian and anti-religious. If she's got negative feelings against Christianity, maybe it's because something bad happened to her. Obviously, in a business office, large religious symbols are not appropriate. You wouldn't walk in with a three-foot statue of Our Lady of Mount Carmel and put it on your desk. There must be proportion. But a small crucifix or a small statue should not trouble anyone. You don't want to add to those negative feelings, so if she asks you to take down a small cross, you could quietly say in an unargumentative way, "Could I ask why it troubles you?" Then you could explain to her that it is very helpful to you, and that you find inspiration in looking at the cross, especially when things are not going too well. That's a reasonable explanation, and it may get a reasonable response from her.

Sixty years ago, I was working in a china shop, and I had a nice picture of the Sacred Heart up over my work bench. My boss saw it, and he was at first kind of amused, but I told him that it meant a whole lot to me. It was fine with my boss to leave it there, and it stayed there for years because my brothers worked in the shop after I did, and they stayed there for fifteen years. You catch more flies with sugar than you do with vinegar: "A spoon full of sugar helps the medicine go down." In this kind of situation, I always think of Mother Teresa's approach. No matter what anyone said to Mother Teresa, even if it was outrageous, she quietly listened and calmly made an answer that she felt was appropriate.

"Why do you have that cross on your desk?" "Because it's the most important symbol in my life." What's somebody going to say? But the tone of voice in which you say it can be the beginning of understanding or the beginning of a battle.

Life after Prison

Please speak about the many problems facing the thousands of men and women released from jails and prisons every year. As a recent parolee, I face many challenges every day. Most are spiritual, concerning the difficulties of rebuilding broken lives. What is our best approach?

Over the years, particularly when I was younger, I did a lot of work with people in prison and people just released from prison. I think that everybody released from prison uses the expression "to hit the streets." It's a feeling of exaltation. "I finally got out of the Rock, and I hit the streets." But there's nothing magical about the streets; rather, they're dangerous and can be unforgiving. The first thing I tell anyone who is on parole or out of prison is "Walk, do not run away from any police car. Don't go around looking for trouble." Unfortunately, people in prison tend often to look for trouble. My impression is many people in prison or who have been in prison were not out to create crime but were falling into obvious trouble and being where they should not have been. I know someone very well who was in a room when people were selling a lot of narcotics. He should not have been there, and he was arrested without any narcotics on him. The police officer claimed he had thrown it out the window. He refused to plead guilty and maintained his innocence. Yet he spent several years in prison.

Also, when you come out of jail, it's too easy to get help from people who are going to hurt you by helping you. Stay away from people who are in trouble or breaking a law or involved in criminal activity. Get an honest job, even if it is not much of a job at all: washing cars or some day-by-day job. Start from there to work your way up gradually. There are many places where people can get a job even if they have a record, and getting started with something very humble, like washing cars, may be the answer. After a person who has been released from prison has made their tough, difficult way for a while, they should ask others to help them do better—not to take care of them but to give them a better chance. And watch out for someone trying to help but accidentally putting something in their way to tempt them—for instance, leaving money around or leaving a safe open. Unfortunately, there are people in prison who, for the moment, can't resist taking money, even though they may not need the money. They even wish they didn't have it, but they have an impulse to grab the money or a car or something.

Stay away from temptation.

Liturgical "Collapse"

I stopped going to church about five years ago because I didn't like the liberalism that was creeping into the Mass. Recently, I moved and decided to go to church again. I was more disappointed than ever. There was no tabernacle and no red candle in the church. Before the Mass began, the priest asked us to introduce ourselves to one another. At the closing of the Mass, he had all who had birthdays come forward and he asked the parishioners to raise their hands in prayer. None of that is part of the Mass. I doubt if I'll go back to that church. Now what do I do?

The first thing I would say is to buy either a car or a bicycle. I'm not just being facetious. This is a day when you can travel, and if the worship services in your local parish are not reverent and awesome, then you should travel. Pope Benedict has said that the key qualities of Catholic liturgy should be reverence and awe, but somehow, not by bad will, a kind of casualness and almost entertainment approach to liturgy has come in. The pope refers to this as "the collapse of the liturgy," and I'm sure he will straighten it out. I'm also sure the parish priest where you are intends only the best to get everybody involved: but involved in what, and how? Don't be too severe in your judgment of him because he may be doing what he was taught to do in the seminary. If you want to be annoyed at people, then be annoyed at people about twenty or thirty years ago who introduced these ideas into the seminary. If I wanted to be unkind, I could give you a list, but I won't do that.

Now, the fact is that you can travel and go to a parish where you feel at home. In the old days, canon law defined your parish geographically, as where you lived. That's no longer the case. In the present canon law, your parish is the one where you regularly go to church and which you regularly support. So you have an opportunity to look around.

I also think it would be a good idea to explain your discomfort to the parish priest. I would do so nicely, because it sounds as if this particular priest, whose identity I don't know, is trying to do his best, but his best is not very good. He appears to be energetic and concerned, but Mass at his parish isn't everybody's cup of tea, and certainly not Pope Benedict's cup of tea. Further, I don't think it fits with the solemn mystery of the Holy Eucharist, the presence of Christ. So speak up, and don't give up.

All who accept the Bible know that the commandment is there to keep holy the Lord's Day. In the Catholic Church, this is defined, among other things, as the obligation to attend Mass on Sunday and not to do unnecessary heavy or servile work. Observing the liturgy on EWTN or some other media is *not* a substitute for attending Mass; it doesn't ordinarily[53] fulfill your obligation, but many elderly, infirm, or housebound people tell me that they get an immense spiritual benefit out of viewing the Mass on EWTN. So there are lots of ways around this problem.

[53] This broadcast far predated the COVID shutdowns, during which Catholics were dispensed from their Sunday obligations for many months. Thus, it is possible for one's bishop to dispense the Sunday Mass obligation in extraordinary circumstances.

Liturgy: Participation of the Laity

It seems to me, because of the shortage of priests, we in the Church have become vulnerable to experimentation in the sense of the laity assuming the role of ordained priests in an attempt to fulfill their own personal desires for leadership, at the expense of the people. Unknown to themselves, they are tampering with the authenticity of our Catholic Faith and being intrusive upon everyone. In my diocese, it seems as if the hierarchy is encouraging such experimentation, unaware of the detrimental effects it has on our faith. I would appreciate very much any advice you could give.

The first thing you should do is study a little history—say, within the last hundred years. Up until that time, the Church was very much run by the clergy. Parish priests, bishops, and cardinals were responsible for the care of people's souls, to lead them, to do pastoral work, to provide sacraments and all that. But in the past, most laypeople did not directly do very much in the life of the Church. There was one group of laypeople, however, who did, and they were the nobility, the aristocracy, who were very much involved in running the Church. This was largely in the Middle Ages, when kings were crowned by bishops, the local lord was installed by the local bishop, and the hierarchies of the Church and of the government kept very close to each other. You can see some leftovers of this in the Anglican Church, which is closely identified with the British government. During the nineteenth century and very clearly in the twentieth century, the Catholic Church departed from those customs. Both Pope Pius X and Pope Pius XI spoke very much of the *lay apostolate*, the ministry of the laity in the Church. In the nineteenth and early-twentieth centuries, there was a great deal of work by groups of lay Catholics called "Catholic Action," some of which are still in existence. In 1905, Pius X issued a whole encyclical on Catholic Action.[54] And so the Church, especially the popes, intended ordinary people to have an important part in the life of the Church.

In some situations, there may be too much influence or too much involvement, but as I read your question, I think that you're wrong. You're leaving out the teaching of the Church in modern times, and especially in the twentieth century, on the lay apostolate. People may be bothered by the laity's involvement in liturgy, but the Church certainly encourages this. Popes Benedict and John Paul II presided at many Masses where there was much lay involvement in the liturgy. I would say that if you went to public liturgies of the popes, you would find more involvement of laypeople in the liturgical life than you would in an ordinary parish or cathedral. And particularly John Paul II, in Africa and in Asia, encouraged people very much to participate as part of the liturgy.

[54] Pope St. Pius X, encyclical *Il Fermo Proposito* (June 11, 1905), https://www.vatican.va/content/pius-x/en/encyclicals/documents/hf_p-x_enc_11061905_il-fermo-proposito.html.

Lourdes

Do you think that Lourdes was a direct answer to the European skeptics and to the atheistic Darwinism that was about to be hatched the next year? That is, instead of sending us a great theologian to explain the biblical miracles, God sent such miracles that could be denied only by denying one's own eyesight.

Of course, I must say that I am a Lourdes person. When I woke up after my accident,[55] I prayed to Our Lady of Lourdes and to St. Bernadette to intercede for me. And I have to say that they have taken good care of me. I'm doing a lot of things that the doctors said I would never do.

It's interesting that you would ask whether it was arranged that way. Who knows? You'd have to ask God. So wait till you get to the Kingdom of Heaven and ask Him if He set this up. It is certainly true that it was timely, not only because of the skepticism of the time, but because of the immense damage that had been done to the Church in France by the French Revolution and, before the Revolution, by the decline and harm that had been done to the Church by many of the bishops who were appointed by the king. The Church in France at that time was a mess. There were bright lights here and there, particularly in religious orders, but much of the Church needed significant reform.

[55] See "Death Experience of Fr. Groeschel," above.

Bernadette, who came from a devout peasant family, was looking for firewood by a little pile of rocks along the river Gave when she, the perfect witness, saw the vision of the Blessed Virgin. Many people, including her family members, were skeptical. For a long time, she would not say she had seen the Blessed Virgin. When people asked her if she had seen the Virgin, she referred to it as *aquerò*, "that." It was during the sixteenth vision that the "small young woman" answered Bernadette, who had several times asked for her name, "I am the Immaculate Conception." Well then, she *had* seen the Blessed Virgin. Bernadette was very cautious. She never added a syllable to her testimony, and she was questioned by very bright clergy, theologians, and canon lawyers. They put her through very serious questioning, and she maintained her wonderful peasant sense of humor.

Because of the healing miracles that took place at Lourdes, immense numbers of people came there, believers and skeptics, Catholics and Protestants, people in need of the help of God who had very serious illnesses. In 1902, Dr. Alexis Carrel, who would later win the Nobel Prize and become the director of Rockefeller University, witnessed a miracle. In his account, *The Voyage to Lourdes*, he says, "I have seen the resurrection of the dead, I have seen a dead woman come back to life," for Marie Bailly was at the shrine on the edge of death. They thought she was going to die, and the doctor told the people not to put her into the waters.

Lourdes had tremendous effects. And it still does. Many books have been written about Lourdes, not all of them written by Catholics or even by believers. But they are very staunch defenders of Lourdes. So it seems to me that this remarkable experience of this fourteen-year-old girl is a perfect example of why God still reveals things to His people to emphasize teachings they already know. Lourdes has made it very clear that God has powers beyond anything that science can seriously pretend to understand.

“Marriage” for Homosexuals

With the movement to legalize gay marriage,[56] what are families to do when one of their children decides to marry and some members choose to accept the marriage as being no different from a traditional marriage? How are they to communicate their love for the couple as individuals without condoning their actions?

This is a good but painful question. I don’t think I’ve ever met anyone who could tell me that they wanted to have same-sex attraction. People who have had such an attraction all their life might say, “Oh well, I like it.” That’s one thing, but I can’t imagine anybody starting out and saying that they would like to have this attraction. You must be careful what words you use, but it is from my way of thinking a misfortune that a person cannot enter a sacramental marriage, cannot have a family in the way that God has chosen for families to naturally exist.

What do we do when people suffer with misfortune? We’re kind to them. We don’t pick on people because they have misfortunes, we don’t call them bad names. I have the misfortune of hobbling around and having a permanently broken arm. I wish I didn’t,

[56] This broadcast predated *Obergefell v. Hodges*, the U.S. Supreme Court decision that legalized gay “marriage.”

but I do have a broken arm, and I do the best I can. And people are kind to me; they help me. Nobody has ever made fun of me because I must hobble around.

Now, the same-sex union is not a marriage. A marriage, according to the Catholic Church, is the wedding of a man and a woman. Whatever else the same-sex union may be, it's perhaps the two people's attempt to normalize their situation as much as they can or to make sure that it lasts. We can understand that. But parents of those in same-sex unions have told me that they are somewhat uncomfortable if they have smaller children or teenagers. Their discomfort is understandable, but on the other hand, they still need to be as compassionate and kind as humanly possible. I think there is a Gospel precedent for this, because Jesus went to people who were considered morally unacceptable: publicans and, as it says, harlots, and He dined with them. Surely, I don't want anybody to write me a letter challenging the fact that I compared same-sex unions to publicans and harlots, because my point is that there was a social stigma attached to those people, and I think Jesus did not make much or anything of social stigmas.

So I would always try to be as kind as possible.

Masons

Some time ago, a person had called in on your show asking about becoming a member of the Masons. You said that the man would have to ask the bishop if that could happen. What about the Masons? And what about a Catholic becoming a member of this organization?

First, let me say that I made a mistake. I know that a Catholic is not allowed to join the Masons. It's very clearly stated, but I was thinking maybe the bishop could give a person a dispensation to do that personally. As a matter of fact, I've checked it out. What I said is not true.

Now, what about the Masons? Most Catholics likely have a few friends who belong to a Masonic lodge. They're your nice next-door neighbors. Different Masonic organizations help people in particular ways. For example, everyone is aware of the work of the Shriners. They are a group of Masons who take care of children who have severe burns, disabilities, things like that. I visited somebody the other day in a nursing home. It was a Masonic nursing home, and about 80 percent of the people working there were Catholics. They're not Masons.

The Masons grew out of a European guild of stonemasons who made their living building stone buildings. Since Europe was essentially all Catholic at this time, it was started by Catholics, and its members were Catholics. So gradually it became a guild *religiously*. However, for two reasons, the Masons got into disfavor with the Church. First, they are a secret order that has a secret or secrets that are apart from the knowledge of the hierarchy and of the Church. Secondly, and sadly, but it must be said, in some places Masons were very vicious in their attacks on the Catholic Church, particularly in Europe and in countries that were essentially Catholic. Probably the worst example is in twentieth-century Mexico. Two presidents of the United States—Woodrow Wilson and Calvin Coolidge—were asked to help stop the violent persecution of the Catholic Church by Mexico's Masonic government, but they did not help. Thousands of priests and more than a dozen bishops were killed. The Mexican Martyrs are several saints who were savagely killed by Masons. Now, of course, none of those Masons are still alive. So there's no good reason to keep up an anti-Masonic operation, and in fact, if you look around, most Masons I've ever met are kind of old like me and rather conservative sorts of people. They certainly are not going around planning on burning down a church. I know one man who lives near EWTN who has been very helpful, sending beautiful flowers to the convent of the sisters.

Because of the history between Masons and the Church, and because we're not able to look at the secret inner rituals of Masons, what can we say? I think that it would be a good move for the Masons to make a movement toward the Church, toward the pope or the bishops, and open the door. You may say that Catholics should do the same thing. But it is the Masons that are a secret society. We don't know what's going on, and when you don't know what's going on, it frightens you. On the other hand, the Catholic Church is the most public organization in the world. Everybody's got an idea about it, believers and unbelievers. It would be better for the Masons to be more open.

So the man who called the show some time ago wanting advice about joining the Masons should realize that the Church does not allow a Catholic to be a member of the Masons.[57]

[57] The Church has, for two centuries, and in various documents issued by fifteen popes, condemned Masonry, also known as Freemasonry. Most recently, and still in force, is the November 26, 1983, document issued by then-Cardinal Ratzinger (now Pope Emeritus Benedict XVI), as head of the Congregation (now Dicastery) for the Doctrine of the Faith, the *Declaration on Masonic Associations*, which forbids Catholics membership in Masonic organizations, "since their principles have always been considered irreconcilable with the doctrine of the Church.... The faithful who enroll in Masonic associations are in a state of grave sin and may not receive Holy Communion."

Mass Intentions

Please talk a little about the term "intentions." I am a new Catholic, and I see in my church's bulletin the names of people who have Mass intentions. Why would the Church single out an individual when offering a Mass?

The fact is that the Church doesn't single out an individual, but the priest himself can single out individuals whom he remembers in a very particular way at the Mass. The Mass is always offered as a prayer to God for the whole world, the whole human race, for all creation, for the Church, and for the people there at Mass. They are all remembered specifically and explicitly. If you listen to the prayers of the Canon, you'll hear that we don't leave anybody out.

Many centuries ago, probably in what are sometimes called the "Dark Ages" during the fifth and sixth centuries, people got the idea of giving a priest an offering—maybe some food, maybe a little money—so that he might remember them very specially in the Mass. This became known as an *intention*. If you belong to a religious order, as I do, you would typically say the intentions that are assigned by the religious community; but twice a month you are free to offer the Mass for any special intentions you have. This is a wonderful way to remember the dead especially but also to remember the living. What a beautiful gift to give a relative, a mother, a father on their birthday—to have a Mass offered for their intention! What a beautiful way to remember the dead. And if you're a new Catholic, you will hear such intentions very frequently. Every year or even every month on the anniversary of a person's death, Mass is offered for them.

You might say, "Well, sometimes they've been at that for twenty-five years. Do they still need prayers along the way?" But remember, the holy souls live on the other side of time, so a Mass that you offer today for a long-deceased person may have assisted them long, long ago, because it's beyond time. Long ago, in our time; "present" for them. This is very mysterious, and it's why people often don't understand the Mass—because it's the one sacrifice of Christ, Who is the one Priest. We priests are just His representatives, and we draw into that great sacrifice of prayer all those for whom we pray.

For example, our monastic community doesn't run parishes, and so none of us get salaries for what we do. We all live on alms: gifts of money, begged food. We hardly ever buy food, and they often give it to us in the market, but most of that goes to the poor, and we ourselves live on alms. Our community now has more than a hundred people who take care of the poor, on whom, last year, we spent more than a million dollars. This includes our hospital for the destitute in Honduras, our shelter at night for the homeless men, the Padre Pio Shelters, the St. Anthony Residence, and several soup kitchens. It's not just our community that provides this assistance, though. We welcome other people to help the poor by helping us. And what do I do in return? Almost every day I offer my Mass especially for everyone who helps us: for all our brothers and sisters in the community, for their parents, their families, for all those who help us, whom we call our benefactors. This very morning, I offered Mass for the deceased members of the Michaels family. These are old friends of mine, and one of them sent me a check and asked me to offer Mass for the family.

It's a beautiful thing to do. Many Jewish people planted trees in memory of loved ones when they first arrived in Israel. Before, it was kind of arid; now it has millions of trees all over the place planted in memory of deceased people. Others do different things: sometimes people build buildings, hospitals, or orphanages, for example. They do something good in memory of the dead. You see these remembrances all over the place.

Catholics particularly, and the Orthodox as well, love to have the liturgy of the Holy Eucharist offered for the deceased. They also offer Masses for the living: for example, for somebody who needs a conversion or for somebody who is very ill. So learn this about Catholicism, and get other people to do it. When I was a kid, to get a Mass intention offered by a priest, you would have to wait several months because the priest had all the Mass intentions taken up for months. There are still Italian parishes where, on January 2, the day they start filling out the Mass intentions for the year, a long line forms at the front door of the church, down the street, made up of people who want to get a Mass said for their mothers on their anniversaries.

I wish the rest of us cared about the dead as much as those Italians do. By the way, if I beat you out of this life, which I probably will, remember me. And know that I'll be praying for you on the other side.

Mass Obligation

What would you say to a person who doesn't want to go to church or thinks that they don't need it? My friend says that he doesn't need the Church in order to praise the Lord. I was shocked when he told me this because he is a Catholic. I tried to say something, but I couldn't find the words to say what I needed to say. Isn't it true that it is a sin not to go unless you have a very good reason not to? What should I tell him?

First, you could tell him that it isn't *our* idea that you should go to church on Sunday; it is God's idea. And it is right there in the Ten Commandments, to keep holy the Lord's Day (Exod. 20:8; Deut. 5:12). This is something that the Hebrew people took extremely seriously. Devout Jews to this day go devoutly to the synagogue or the temple on Saturday, their Lord's Day. The Apostles decided that they would pray together on Sunday because that was the day of the week on which Christ rose from the dead.

You can also tell your friend that the obligation to pray in public is recognized not simply by Christians and Jews but by every major religion in the world. He's turning his back not only on the Gospel and on the Bible but on the experience of billions of religious people in the world who believe that they have an obligation to thank their Creator and to acknowledge, as St. Paul says in the first chapter of the Epistle to the Romans, "his eternal power and deity" (Rom. 1:20).

When your friend says that he prays by himself, that's very good. You should pray yourself, but if you read the Gospel, the Epistles, and the Old Testament, you will see that we are called to pray as a community. The Church is a community of charity, an *ekklesía*, a people "called out together." The very earliest Christians met in *synagogues*, "assemblies," which were Jewish places of worship. But under these circumstances, your friend is neither encouraging nor receiving encouragement from all the other people who want to pray together; he's off by himself. It is very healthy to belong to a religious group for support, for instruction, and for correction. If you belong to a decent congregation and you're out of line, they'll tell you.

If this man knew what the Holy Eucharist was, the Holy Sacrifice of the Mass, given to us by Christ the night before His death, commanding us to "Do this in remembrance of me" (Luke 22:19), receiving Christ's Body and Blood, maybe he would not want to be on his own. I love the Holy Sacrifice of the Mass. It's the very center of my life. Eternity, absolute Infinity, breaks into my life whenever I look at that Host and at the chalice of wine and when I say the words of Christ: "This is my Body; this is my Blood. Do this in memory of me." If I lost everything else, but I had that, I would hold on to that as the most important thing of my life.

Your friend is not a priest, but he is a member of the Church, and he should be receiving Holy Communion. You might ask him: Can he give himself Holy Communion? Can he forgive his own sins? Christ said to the Apostles, who were His first clergy, "If you forgive the sins of any, they are forgiven" (John 20:23). This wasn't my idea. In my life, I've heard many thousands of confessions. It wasn't a lot of fun; it was the same old stuff over and over again. But hearing it was fulfilling what Christ said to do.

St. Paul wrote to the Philippians, "It is my prayer that your love may abound more and more, with knowledge and all discernment, so that you may approve what is excellent, and may be pure and blameless for the day of Christ" (Phil. 1:9–10). He's talking about something that must take place in community together. Over and over, page after page, epistle after epistle, this same Paul, the founder of so many churches, calls the people to come together, that they should pray and keep growing more and more together in the knowledge and love of Christ. I feel sorry for your friend, and I think you should feel sorry for him, because he's missing one of the most beautiful and important things of his life.

Mother Elvira

I would like to hear both your spiritual and psychological opinions of the work undertaken by Mother Elvira in her community. They have a radical approach to addiction that seems out of step with mainstream treatment programs. My son entered the community in May of this year. I eagerly testify to the miracle that I witnessed toward the healing of my son. In this regard, I often quote that famous passage from the Gospel of Luke: "This son of mine was dead and has come to life again" (15:24).

Mother Elvira is a remarkable nun. Starting with the Comunità Cenacolo in Italy, and now having cenacles in the United States and several other countries, she receives people suffering from drug and alcohol addiction. The word *cenacle* (*cenacolo*), which means "dining room," refers also to the Upper Room where Jesus celebrated the Last Supper. By extension, it can also refer to a prayer room.

Mother Elvira is the type of person who doesn't take no for an answer. I have never met her, but I think she's probably cut from the same piece of cloth as Mother Teresa and Mother Angelica. She began this ministry with a basic prayer program directed toward the reform of Christian life that has helped thousands of young people like the questioner's son get their life straightened out and cleaned up.

The questioner seems to think that this radical approach is out of step with mainstream treatment programs. I wouldn't say it's out of step; I'd say it's a couple of steps ahead. Treatment programs, if they're successful, take a strong point of view: shape up or ship out; behave, if you want to be here, and no more shenanigans. There are many agencies to deal with alcohol addiction, drug addiction, and all of them that I know that are successful are "shape-up-or-ship-out" programs. Behave or leave! Mother Elvira just took this a couple of steps further and said, "You're going to listen to the Gospel, and if you don't want to, there's the door." All successful programs make a person come to a daily decision about themselves. Right off the bat this gives a person some self-respect, which they may not have had for many years. They suddenly realize they're not just a pawn of their own desires; they're not just an accident waiting to happen.

Mother Elvira, of course, comes in with the "heavy equipment" of the Gospel. Other such programs don't have this. AA and many twelve-step programs encourage people to use their religious values, but they're not religious organizations. Many of them will say that they are spiritual organizations, but Mother Elvira, being a Catholic, running a Catholic program, doesn't have to make any bones about it at all. I would say that she, along with her many associates, must do an exceptionally good job of confronting people with the saving message of Our Lord Jesus Christ.

Mother Teresa and Princess Diana

I was wondering, do you know anything about Mother Teresa's meeting with Princess Diana?

Oh yes, I sure do. Mother Teresa was visited by Princess Diana Spencer about a year before their deaths, I believe. They died within a week of each other. Diana died tragically in a car accident on August 31, 1997. Mother Teresa peacefully went home to God a few days later, on September 5.

Princess Diana was very interested in the poor and in the work that Mother Teresa was doing for them. She came to the South Bronx, to 145th Street, and she had a long talk with Mother Teresa. I never asked, but I'm assuming that she must have left something to help the sisters with their work. If I had asked, nobody would have told me.

Mother Teresa did not see Diana as a princess. When she spoke of her, she called her "child." She would say, "Oh yes, that child came to see me." Mother Teresa was very old, and when she called you "child," it was a term of great affection.

Most people don't know this, but Princess Diana has a relative who has been proposed for canonization: the Venerable Ignatius Spencer, who was a Passionist Father, an English convert around the time Cardinal Newman was received into the Church by another Passionist, blessed Dominic Barberi.[58]

Now, I'm quite sure that Princess Diana was not a Catholic, but obviously some of her family were converts to the Catholic Church.

[58] This is a part of the beautiful tradition of the Passionists. Another one of that congregation, the Dutchman Charles of Mount Argus, who ministered in Dublin, Ireland, is about to be canonized. [In fact, Charles of Mount Argus, also known as Charles Houben of St. Andrew, was canonized on June 3, 2007.]

Muslims

In the last few years, Pope Benedict has reached out in a kindly way to people and leaders of the Muslim nations. This is a bit confusing because we have had attacks like 9-11 by Muslim extremists. One does see mosques around in the United States. What is the best attitude to have toward Muslim people in our country since there are large numbers of them at the present time?

I very much regret the fact that the media, which does have to report the news about Muslim extremists, tells you very little about a much larger number of law-abiding decent Muslim citizens. There are startlingly large numbers of Muslims in the United States. Recently, I read an amazing statistic that there were more Muslims than there were Jewish people in the United States.

You see mosques here and there, but the people who go to these mosques are not conspiring to blow up the railroad. Unfortunately, law-abiding, peaceful, respectable Muslims are very embarrassed and humiliated right now. I always reach out to them. The Franciscans and the Muslims have gotten along very well in the Holy Land for centuries. When the Crusaders had to leave the Holy Land and the Muslims took over, they never sent the Franciscans away, and we're still there after eight hundred years. Interestingly enough, I have met laypeople who are Latin Rite Catholics from families that came from Jerusalem, the Holy Land, and they have lived there since the time of the Crusades.

I think it would be a very good thing for Christians to extend themselves to an honest, law-abiding Muslim person and let them know that we understand that they're doing their best. Look through Church history: Catholic, Protestant, and Orthodox. There have been times when some people in these denominations did violent things too. So we're all part of this. Give young Muslims an example of Christians and Jews who can be kind and understanding to them. It's a very good suggestion.

"Only Son of God"

I have a problem with using the title "only Son of God" as a dogmatic test of a person's faith in Christ. My understanding is that we are all created in the image of God.

In the sense that we are created in the image of God (Gen. 1:26–27), all human beings are children of God. But there's another sense of this expression: Jesus Himself personally speaks about *becoming* children of God, for instance, in the Sermon on the Mount (Matt. 5:9). This latter designation by Jesus indicates people who are, as we would say, in the grace of God: they have drawn close to God; they are receiving His help; they are receiving His divine life. That's incredibly important.

More to the point, however, my friend who wrote this question is saying, I think, "Look, I have the grace of God. So then I am a child of God." This is true. However, Jesus Christ is the *only-begotten* Son of God (John 3:16). "Begotten" here does not refer to the natural process of reproduction. Rather, it refers to the revealed truth that the almighty eternal Father gave His entire being without any restraint to His eternal divine Son, such that the Son and the Father share the same nature. This is what Jesus means when He says, "I and the Father are one" (John 10:30) and "He who has seen me has seen the Father" (John 14:9). The great apologist Frank Sheed went through the Gospels and found 235 examples of Christ directly or indirectly claiming to be in that utterly unique relationship with God or to be divine. Jesus repeatedly indicates a very special relationship that He has with God the Father that no one else has.

Original Sin

I am confused about the relationship between the doctrine of Original Sin and the freedom of the will. If there is a force within us that pulls us toward that which is evil, even when we know that we are acting against conscience and good sense, as St. Paul seems to indicate in one of his epistles, doesn't that severely limit our capacity to make free choices? And if that is so, how culpable are we for our sins? It seems apparent to me that freedom of the will, if it exists, is very limited indeed. Einstein, quoting Schopenhauer, said that a man can do what he wants, but he cannot choose what he wants. I hope you can clear this one up for me.

If I could clear that one up for you, I want to tell you, I would retire immediately after it and bask in the light of all the adoring publicity.

You've asked a very big question. Nobody ever faced the question quite as directly as St. Paul. In Romans 7, he lamented, "For I do not do what I want, but I do the very thing I hate.... It is no longer I that do it, but sin which dwells within me.... Who will deliver me from this body of death?" (Rom. 7:15–24). Later in the same epistle, Paul says that the law of Christ will deliver us—that is, the law of love (Rom. 13:8).

How it all fits together, I don't know. It's perfectly obvious that human beings have some freedom; many have a good deal of freedom. What they set out to do, they do. It's also perfectly obvious that many human beings have little freedom. Drug addicts don't make up their mind to stay clean for a day, as you do in AA. They must make up their mind to stay clean for the next minute. That's how little freedom they have. But many of them try, and I have seen people get over substantial addictions to intravenous cocaine, which is incredible. They did this by prayer; by confession, telling their faults to others; by doing good things; and by reliance on God because they knew that they were powerless. I know people who were on the edge of death and, little by little, gained the freedom to overcome this horror. You should rather be bound by iron chains than by cocaine.

On the other side, there is the fact that even the best of us know that we do stupid things. You may be trying to lead a very good and holy life, and yet you still do stupid things. I've heard the confessions of people who are probably going to be canonized saints. They had no trouble finding things to go to Confession about, because without ever really wanting to do something sinful, they knew that they failed here or there by vanity, by self-love, by a lack of generosity, by anger, or by annoyance. I've personally had two canonizable saints slightly annoyed at me in my life: Blessed [now St.] Mother Teresa and the Venerable [now Blessed] Fr. Solanus. Each got just a little annoyed at me, and I suppose I deserved it. And I want to tell you, when you get somebody like that annoyed at you just a little, it doesn't feel so good. I felt like I had been harpooned by Captain Ahab.

None of us has absolute freedom, and the drama goes on. At one time in your life, you may have more than at another time. Who knows? Only one person must know: God. Now, when we priests hear confessions, we're supposed to help a person come to an understanding of their own responsibility and sin. You do the best you can, but we all know that human beings are weak and tempted and haunted by weaknesses that come to them out of their childhood. There are statements like, "Work like it depended on you, and trust God like it depends on Him." I don't find that too helpful because I never thought it depended completely on me, and I can't fool myself. My motto is "Take the next good step." Whoever you are, whatever your problems, and there are addicts listening to me right now: take the next good step. And the next good step is: *don't set yourself up for evil.*

You know, St. Augustine was a sexual addict before his conversion. He didn't know what to do, but he knew he would find the answer in the Bible. He threw open the Bible and came to these words in Paul's Epistle to the Romans: "Let us conduct ourselves becomingly as in the day, not in reveling and drunkenness, not in debauchery and licentiousness, not in quarreling and jealousy. But put on the Lord Jesus Christ, and make no provision for the flesh, to gratify its desires" (Rom. 13:13–14). *Make no provision for the flesh.* Don't set yourself up, don't have the occasions of sin around. Take the next good step.

The Orthodox Church

I am Greek Orthodox, and I am truly humbled by your respect of other religions and of Orthodoxy, which I find many people know so little about. My question is, do you think that there is a true desire for the unity of the Catholic and the Orthodox churches?

I don't think there's any doubt that there is a desire and that it is growing. As a young priest, I was trained to serve Mass in the Rite of St. John Chrysostom, also called the Byzantine Rite, as it exists in the Ruthenian Greek Catholic Church. That great priest Fulton J. Sheen had earlier obtained permission to offer Mass in the Byzantine Rite, which is the most widely used of several Eastern rites. Ukrainian, Ruthenian, and Melkite Catholics, Greek Orthodox, Russian Orthodox, and many others, both Catholic and Orthodox, use the Rite of St. John Chrysostom, archbishop of Constantinople. It is a very beautiful rite, and if you've never been to a Byzantine Rite Mass or an Orthodox Divine Liturgy, you should go.

Now, in reality, the Orthodox and the Catholics were one church up until about 1400. They divided for many reasons and over a long period of time, partially because of the misbehavior of one group of Crusaders who sacked Constantinople on their way to the Near East to defend the Holy Land. Because of that, there was the Great Schism. There were also, initially, a few theological disagreements, which historically have been exaggerated.

Let's wait and see what God has in mind. The Holy Father Pope John Paul II referred to the Orthodox church and the Catholic Church as the two lungs of the Mystical Body of Christ. I don't know where we're going to put the Protestants because they're also Christians.

The Poem of the Man-God and Private Revelation

What do you think about The Poem of the Man-God *by Maria Valtorta?*

What I am going to tell you about Ms. Valtorta I got from the publishers of the Italian edition of her book. Her *Poem of the Man-God* is a very long meditation on the life of Christ written in clear language, rather well written literarily. It brings into the story all kinds of details, side issues, explanations, and other things that are not in the Gospels, canonical or apocryphal. Ms. Valtorta presented this as a revelation given to her. It should be known that Ms. Valtorta—who was very devout—according to her Italian publishers, fell into an extremely serious psychological difficulty. She really could not function at all.

I read some passages in *The Poem of the Man-God*, and I would have to tell you that I did see the edges of things, phenomena that I would associate with the beginnings of mental illness. Cardinal Ratzinger, now Pope [Emeritus] Benedict XVI, condemned the book very strongly, when he was prefect of the Congregation for the Doctrine of the Faith, and even referred to it as a lump of theological absurdities. I know that some people have been very moved by this book, and so I would say, if you read it, don't read it like Scripture. These are the meditations of a devout and gifted woman who was slipping into mental illness. If you keep that in mind, then it might present some ideas to you.

The Pope and the People

When Pope Benedict visited New York recently, I saw youngsters on television embracing the pope when he was at the seminary. I never saw anything like that before in my life, and I don't think it is respectful. Are things changing with the pope?

Yes, things are changing, and what are changing are the social customs surrounding the bishop of Rome. This is very interesting because I was present for this and noticed it myself. During the Middle Ages, the popes were the rulers of a country, the Papal States. They had to take their place with the kings and queens of Europe. Charlemagne himself made it clear that the pope was above the Holy Roman Emperor. Charlemagne received the crown from Pope Leo III on Christmas Day in the year 800.

In Chinese, the word for "pope" is "emperor of religion." Throughout the Middle Ages, people showed to popes the same honors that they showed to kings and emperors. This continued right up into modern times along with various kingly appointments, including the pope's crown, the tiara, and the *sedia gestitoria*, the seat on which the pope sat and was carried, on the shoulders of men, when he went out into the crowds in St. Peter's Square. Beginning with Pope John XXIII, Pope Paul VI, and especially Pope John Paul II, the popes put aside gradually but not dramatically 95 percent of those things. The royal trappings are gone, including the crown. Now the pope comes not as a king, not as the president, not as a politician but as a shepherd and father, often in the "popemobile." I couldn't be happier.

In New York, I was watching Pope Benedict when the first little girl came up to him on stage. I think she did it spontaneously; she threw her arms around the pope, and he seemed to be delighted. As each person came up, he opened his arms. He is the shepherd, the father of the Church, though Pope Benedict, who is six years older than I am, comes off a little bit like the grandfather of the Church. That's wonderful. I see no problem with that in terms of the Holy Gospel and in terms of the Acts of the Apostles and the work of St. Peter. Goodbye to the imperial papacy and hello to the spiritual father of the human race.

Prayer and God's Answer

I'm a seventeen-year-old Catholic. While reading the Gospels, I have been troubled by certain promises of Christ—namely, "Whatever you ask in My name, I will do it. That the Father may be glorified in the Son" and also "Ask, and it shall be given to you, seek and you will find, knock and it will be open to you." These are only two of several places in the Gospels where He makes these promises. Jesus gives us here no reservations or conditions to these promises. Here, He does not even add "if you have faith" or "if you ask the things I want you to ask for." He simply tells us to ask for anything in His name, but can He really mean this? I don't mean to be disrespectful, but these promises are so extravagant and seemingly unfulfilled in so many cases that I simply don't know what to make of them. Are there, in reality, only certain things we are allowed to ask for in reference to these promises?

This is one of the very burning questions for the believer because we are told to trust God, and obviously things go wrong. Think of all the people in Europe who prayed that the Communists, the Bolsheviks, and the Nazis would not take over. Yet they did. Think even of the Blessed Virgin Mary, when her Son was arrested, how she must have prayed that each of those events in the Passion wouldn't happen: His scourging, His being crowned with thorns, His carrying of the Cross, His Crucifixion and death. But they did happen. The Church associates with Our Lady a verse from the Old Testament: "Is it nothing to you, all you who pass by? Look and see if there is any sorrow like my sorrow" (Lam. 1:12). And so the question is very real.

Now, the first consideration is that, obviously, God could not be putting the control of the world into our hands. The material world follows laws—thermodynamics, gravity, and so forth. These laws continue in operation, unless, in a very rare case, they may be miraculously suspended. There are examples of this in the New Testament. For example, Christ spoke to the sea, and it calmed down. When they witnessed this, the Apostles said, "What sort of man is this, that even winds and sea obey Him?" (Matt. 8:27). That kind of thing doesn't happen very often, but what if you study these quotations our questioner mentioned, with which I am quite familiar. We learn that we are promised that we will be answered. It may not be the answer we want, but it will be the answer we need, the answer that leads to eternal life. It takes faith to accept that. You pray that someone dearly loved by others won't die, and yet they die. What happened to God? But in the course of time, you see that by the providence of God, those things you prayed for have taken shape in a new way, and good comes out of evil. My own experience with the car accident[59] and the suffering and multiple near-death episodes: I might wish it happened a different way, but at this point I don't wish—I couldn't wish—that it didn't happen because it made me who I am today. I would be a different person without that accident. A lot of good things happened because of that accident. I had a dear friend who was a Polish priest who spent four and a half years in Auschwitz and Dachau. And he said the same thing: that he can't wish that it

[59] See "Death Experience of Fr. Groeschel," above.

hadn't happened because it made him who he was. So God brings good out of evil. When we accept this, we use not only the virtue of faith but the next virtue in line, which is hope: that amid all the difficulties of life, God will bring good out of it. If you're not a believer, that sounds crazy.

One of the most horrible events in the twentieth century was the Holocaust. Whenever I go to Jerusalem, I go to the Holocaust Museum, the Yad Vashem. The last time I went, there was a beautiful, big white marble building, the Children's Museum. I thought, "Lord, deliver me. I can't look at this. There's going to be baby shoes; there's going to be pictures of little children killed." But finally I went in. It was the most unusual exhibit I've ever seen. It was all mirrors arranged from floor to ceiling, as mirrors used to be in what we call the maze or the Fun House at the amusement park. Wherever you turned you saw white candles burning. They tell me there are just a few white candles burning in the building. But the mirrors are so arranged that every step you take, you're surrounded by what look to be hundreds, thousands of white burning candles. It's a marvelous work of art. And each one of those candles is a symbol of a human soul. It's a great Monument to Hope, and I wish that everybody in the world could see it because it represents the most dark and sinister and iniquitous evil, the killing of innocent children. And in the Children's Museum of the Yad Vashem, it is converted into hope.

You and I have been praying for years for the end of abortion. We don't seem to be getting too far. But when we get on the other side, don't worry about the children, for the universal saving will of God will take care of those innocent children. The people to worry about are the people who will look into the face of God, and for human reasons, say, "I will not serve." I'm not talking about the people who are sincerely pro-death, or pro-abortion. (I won't call them "pro-choice" because life is a choice.) I've talked to some of those people; they are honestly deceived. Some of them are people of goodwill. It's the other people who say, "Well, I know it's wrong, but I've got to go along with the crowd" who may find themselves on the Last Day in a very untenable position.

Now, in the middle of all this, you pray. If this is hard for you to hear, I have a group of people who can teach you. Go into the poorest section of any large city, and you will find living there prayerful women who know what Jesus teaches about prayer. In the Bronx, I knew some dear holy old black ladies. These were ladies who lived most of their lives with segregation. They were peaceful, beautiful, humble, and prayerful. They can teach you what those words of Jesus [that the questioner quoted] mean. There was a little storefront church near us, and sometimes on Wednesday evening, I would look in if I was coming by before the prayer meeting. Several old grandmothers would be there, a couple of old grandfathers, a few kids. They would see me look in and say, "Oh, hello brother, how are you, brother?" I had a game I played with them. I'd say one word, and I'd get the answer right back. When I would say my favorite word, *ask*, they would immediately reply, "And you shall receive." "*Seek* and you shall find; *knock*, and it shall be opened unto you." How blessed are the poor in spirit. How blessed are they that hunger and thirst for justice.

Prayer Requests

Since they are so common these days, are online prayer requests considered prayer?

First, I wouldn't know how to turn on a computer. The friars don't have computers, and I'm not even sure what the expression *online* means! I do know that I can order plane tickets online because I'm always flying here and there to preach, but I don't book them myself. So, I assume that *online* means that people must e-mail others, asking them to pray for them. That would not be a prayer, but certainly the person who is responding can pray. I do know that when I was recovering from the car accident four years ago, fifty thousand people sent me promises of their prayer. Fifty thousand people! And the machine somehow or other kept all those addresses. And when I got better, all I had to do was write one little note, somebody pressed a button, and all fifty thousand people got my thank-you note. It's a great idea, but it's beyond me!

I'm a man of another age, and I would say that using an online prayer request is not a prayer. The computer can't pray. You can put prayers on a photograph or a tape recorder. They're still not prayers. Prayer is the lifting up of the heart and mind to God, and you've got to have a heart and mind to do it. But it is a good way to get people to pray.

Prayer: Intercessory Value for the Dead

I have been praying the Rosary nearly every day. I try to do this every single day for a young college student who committed suicide last year. I don't know why I do this; I never knew this boy, but I feel compelled to do so. Do my prayers have any intercessory value? I know they have value for me anyway, but I'm hoping that there is hope for this boy who was Catholic. Thank you and God bless.

I'm very impressed that you are praying so fervently for someone you don't know; that is a real act of charity. Our Savior tells us in the Gospels in several parables to make incessant prayer; not to make long, long prayers but rather to be persistent in prayer. In the parable of the importunate neighbor, the neighbor importuned is in bed, but because the importunate neighbor keeps banging on his door, he gives him what he needs. Jesus then says, "And I tell you, ask, and it will be given you; seek, and you will find; knock, and it will be opened to you" (Luke 11:5–9). Why do we have to tell God what to do? Because Our Lord tells us to do that. It's the parable of the unjust judge (Luke 18:1–8). The judge gives the old widow her rights because she's driving him crazy. Our Lord suggests that kind of prayer.

Now, strictly speaking, you can't pray for someone who is lost, nor can you pray for someone who is in Heaven because they don't need our prayers. But in certain places in the New Testament there are references to prayers for the dead, and Jews still pray the Kaddish prayer for the dead. Now, suppose the boy, God forbid, is lost or, God be praised, has eternal life in Heaven. Still, the prayers for this person are not wasted; in God's wisdom, they will be directed toward other people who need those prayers. I think of Pope John Paul speaking about aborted children, who are not baptized. He said that we must never give up hope. Therefore, many of my friends and I pray that God, in His infinite mercy, will bring these little innocent, defenseless children into His kingdom just as He brought the Holy Innocents, the children in Bethlehem killed by King Herod, whom the Church has always recognized as saints. Remember, God wills the salvation of the world. When we pray, we're not pulling it out of Him, or making Him face up to a tough bargain. He wishes the salvation of souls more than we do. But it is the teaching of the Bible and of the Church that when we die, we render an account of our lives to God.

I read that 94 percent of the American people believe in a personal God, and something like 89 or 87 percent believe that at the end of your life, you render an account of your works. Therefore, there are many people in the world today who are apt to believe that such prayers for the dead are effective. I pray every day, in the Mass and my other prayer, for all who will die that day, for all the souls on their way to God, and especially for those who have had difficult and tragic lives, like this poor young man.

Prayer and Thinking

How does one know if one is praying and not merely thinking?

This is a very interesting question. I've been writing and talking about the spiritual life for many years, and this is the first time I've had anyone ask that intelligent question. How do you know if you're praying or thinking? Well, what is prayer? It is the lifting up of the heart and mind to God. Now, if our thoughts are thoughts of God, or thoughts about our relationship with God, or about doing the work of God, then it seems to me they are a kind of prayer. However, if our thoughts are just about, for example, planning ecclesiastical things, they might not be prayers, though they might be good thoughts. For instance, you're running a reception in the church to raise money for new fire extinguishers, and you're planning that out and whom you should ask to come. That's a good work, but it's not a prayer. However, if you're honestly praying about how some good thing can be done and asking the Lord, especially the Holy Spirit, to guide you, then that's a prayer.

I had a very challenging situation last year. I was visiting the Carthusian hermits in an old monastery in Parkminster, England. The Carthusians are a very austere order, and they're hermits. They spend most of their day alone. They pray the divine office together, but they eat alone; they're alone all day. They may come together for Mass; sometimes they say Mass alone, sometimes together, and once a week for a few hours, they go for a long walk, rain or shine. They're very devout and deeply prayerful men. You may have seen the movie *Into Great Silence*. It's about the Carthusians.

So, there I am visiting the Carthusians, and they want me to give them a talk—sixty of them—but what am I going to talk to Carthusians about? Contemporary trends in pastoral counseling or something? So I prayed to the Holy Spirit: I went into the chapel, and I said, "Listen, I've got to talk to these guys, Holy Spirit. You better put the words on my lips because I'm in over my head." And as I was walking along, two of my favorite words came into my mind: "be led." "The LORD is my shepherd, I shall not want; he makes me lie down in green pastures" (Ps. 23:1–2). He leadeth me. So I gave them a talk about letting yourself be led, and I tried to fit it into the Carthusian life.

Think about it: a man goes away to become a contemplative monk, and he's there in his little Carthusian cell and he can't pray, his heart is like a stone, his mind is either a blank or filled with distractions. Such an experience happened to Mother Teresa. If you and I can't pray, we can go do something good, or take a walk, or listen to EWTN. We can do a lot of things. The Carthusian has no place to go, and so they must be led. They have put themselves in a position that only God can lead them. So I gave my little talk, very intimidated, and I found out later that the Carthusians thought it was the greatest thing since strawberry shortcake. They loved it. Why? Because it was the work of the Holy Spirit. That's why. It wasn't anything I cooked up; I hardly prepared it at all, I didn't even know what I was doing.

Be led. And when you pray, think where your thoughts are leading you. What are they telling you? Even your distractions: if you're trying to pray and you're distracted by something, stop and look at what's distracting you. If you're thinking about what you are going to do on your next day off, it could be telling you that you're too wrapped up in days off; or that you do need a day off; or that you need to spend your day off doing something better; or that you're going to do your day off well and visit some persons who need to be visited. Discern what it is that your thoughts are saying.

Then there is direct prayer, where we speak to God or we speak to Our Lady or to one of the saints. When you get finished speaking to them, consider what you said. If we could hear a recording of our prayers, I think most of us would know that we must do better. There's lots of room for improvement, and never be afraid to find out that you have a need for improvement in your spiritual life.

Jesus says, "Follow me." He never says, "Sit down because you're there." In Christianity, you're never there: you're moving.

Priests: How to Encourage Them

I have heard reference to "the Year of the Priest." What can you suggest parishioners do to help and encourage their parish priest daily?

It's unfortunate that, when the Year of the Priest was announced, it did not get very much attention. I believe it was declared by the pope himself, and certainly it has been an encouragement to a great many priests. With the scandal that came, the vast majority of the clergy, who had nothing at all to do with it, were shocked and deeply pained by the whole thing.[60]

On top of that, there is an obvious chilling of respect for any state of life. There is not much respect for marriage or for other people who have important positions—physicians, for example. So, some group of people must have suggested that there be a "year for priests." For thirty-six years, my full-time job has been to work with priests. I run a retreat house for priests. Over the years, I've counted it up. I've given more than a thousand retreats to priests. And I have also helped with priests who were coming back into the priesthood after they had had a time of difficulty and crisis—almost fifty of those. I am so pleased and grateful to God for that.

[60] Fr. Groeschel likely is referring to the Archdiocese of Boston sexual abuse scandal.

I also help priests who leave the priesthood. Many leave it, sadly. They know, for different reasons, that they can't live up to the requirements of the priesthood, and so they leave. But when they meet me, and I always show respect to them and to their wives and their children, there's always a little look in their eye, you know. He was a priest, and every priest knows that he is still a priest. When a priest leaves the priesthood, he gets a letter from the Vatican that dispenses him from celibacy and gives permission to get married, and it also says he can do no functions as a priest, except, if someone is in danger of death, he can give the sacraments, hear confessions, and, if he could get the Blessed Sacrament, bring the Blessed Sacrament to them and give them the Holy Anointing. So right there in the letter from the Vatican is that exception. It reminds us all that "once a priest, always a priest." Now people talk about what to do for the priests. Fortunately for me, the same year turned out to be my fiftieth anniversary as a priest.

On my fiftieth anniversary as a priest, I tried to play it very quietly, but people didn't comply with my wishes, and so I'm very happy that all those gifts for me were given to the work with the poor, especially the Good Counsel Homes for homeless mothers and their babies. The others we gave to the superior of the community. I didn't even get a dinner out of the whole thing because I wanted to celebrate by giving things to other people. I should say that two of my friends then took me out to a little Italian restaurant, and we had a nice dinner. But nobody talked about my fiftieth. How do I feel about having been a priest for fifty years? Immensely grateful to God. I'm safe to talk about it now because all the celebrations are over. I'm still getting cards in the mail, and I'm looking forward to my fifty-first anniversary so I don't have to celebrate anything. But I am immensely grateful to God to be a priest.

I knew when I was seven years old that I was supposed to be a priest, even though I wanted to be a fireman. I didn't want to be a priest, but I was praying in church as a little kid, and there went the firehouse and there I am a priest. I was a priest when I was very young, twenty-five years old, and the Jewish secretary I had years ago said that I was born a priest. I'm so happy and grateful to God for making me a priest, but it's hard work to be a good priest: you've got to work, and you must be able to sacrifice yourself, your feelings and such things. Because priests are unmarried, they have much more time free than other clergymen. I knew a wonderful Presbyterian minister, a great man, one of whose youngsters, unfortunately, died of an overdose. Many Catholic priests and sisters came to the funeral, and I approached him and told him how terribly sorry I was for him. He replied, "You know, I neglected my family." He did because he was working so hard, such an excellent minister. But how do you balance that? He was an outstanding clergyman. To this day, I pray for him and his wife.

So I'm happy to be a priest, and I'm happy to be a clergyman, working for the Kingdom of God, and to give the wonderful sacraments of Holy Communion and absolution. The most beautiful is the Eucharist, but the most meaningful is Confession. I'll say if I had a choice of losing my eyesight or my hearing, I would choose to lose my eyesight so I could still hear confessions, because that's the wonderful, beautiful lifting of sins off another person's soul.

So the Lord put me here in the Year of the Priest, and I'm very grateful to God for being here.

Priests: When They Are in Error

We get many inquirers who feel that they have been told things by priests that are inaccurate or leave them spiritually unsettled. This is particularly true of people who confess sins that are dismissed by the confessor as not being sins. There may be other cases where priests say things that are contrary to the teachings of the Church, which is particularly true regarding the subject of Christ. What should we do in such situations?

You do *not* have to listen and you *should not* listen to someone—priest, bishop, anybody else—who is misrepresenting the teaching of the Church. Period. When I was growing up, there was a saying, "Father knows best," a very Irish Catholic saying. But in those days, priests were very careful never to say anything that wasn't the teaching of the Church. The thought never crossed our minds, and it never crossed my mind when I was ordained a priest in 1959. But in the confusion after the Vatican Council,[61] and especially the confusion of the 1970s and 1980s—which spiritually was a very dark time for all believers in the United States—in that confusion, people were taught the wrong things and arrived at wrong conclusions. For instance, I am outraged when I hear someone

[61] The Second Vatican Council (Vatican II), which convened periodically from 1962 to 1965.

say that Christ did not know who He was. This undermines the basic teaching of the Catholic Church, the Orthodox church, and most Protestant churches. I've seen this up close because I've been teaching in the seminary for forty-five years. I saw a tremendous amount of confusion come in, and I was in the middle of the battles and suffered many wounds.

So Jesus Christ is a divine Person. That understanding is given and binding from the Council of Ephesus (AD 431), from the Council of Chalcedon (451), and following the teaching of Pope Leo the Great. To say that a divine Person doesn't know who He is is absurd; it's preposterous. How Christ's human knowledge and His divine knowledge fit together and interplayed with each other certainly is absolutely mysterious. It's not even a psychological question because psychology is based on data gathered from examples, and there are no other examples of anyone who was a God-man, because there is only one. In other words, Christ's psychology is inaccessible to us. The great theologian Msgr. Romano Guardini, in his book *The Humanity of Christ: Contributions to a Psychology of Jesus*,[62] tears to pieces these opinions, such that for someone to get up and apodictically say without qualification that Christ did not know who He was is, to me, to undermine the faith of the faithful. It is to do something very wrong, and I know people whose faith, even this year, was undermined by such statements by a scholar.

The Scriptures, however, bear a different witness. For example, as a twelve-year-old child, Jesus says to His parents, "Did you not know I must be in my Father's house?" (Luke 2:49). And Jesus mentions or implies several times His oneness with the Father.[63]

62 Trans. Ronald Walls (Cluny Media, 2018).

63 E.g., John 10:30: "I and the Father are one"; John 14:9: "He who has seen me has seen the Father"; Luke 10:22: "All things have

If you want to ignore all these statements, my suggestion is to get out of Christianity. If you try to shoot holes in the Gospel and call it the Word of God while you treat it like the words of men, then quit. We'll see if we can find some Unitarian Church for you to join up with. They'll be nice to you. But get out of Christianity. Don't be a phony Christian. I'd rather an authentic Unitarian than a phony Christian any day of the week.

Unfortunately, you do find priests who are like this: badly trained, badly educated. Speak to them kindly and point out that what they are saying is uncalled for and unhelpful. And if they won't listen, tell them to get in touch with me; I'll be happy to talk to them on the phone. I'm apodictic about this. If I were sitting in Church and the priest got up and said Jesus didn't know who He was, I would get up and walk out right then. *Finito e basta!* Keep your greasy lunch grabbers off Jesus Christ. That's from Jersey City.

As for when a priest hears confessions, he hears them as a representative of Christ and of His Church. It is true that some people think things are sins that are not. There are some people who don't recognize the effects that human weakness can have on human freedom. But to cavalierly dismiss sins that people feel guilty about is to be a bad confessor.

We live in tough times. May I ask you to pray for priests? It is a very difficult time to be a priest, and I encourage every priest who's listening to find his refuge in being a loyal representative and loyal son of the Catholic Church.

been delivered to me by my Father; and no one knows who the Son is except the Father, or who the Father is except the Son and any one to whom the Son chooses to reveal him."

Private Revelations

There are many reports of private revelations, especially of Our Lady speaking to people. Should we take these seriously and let them guide our lives?

Private revelation is a very big subject, and so I'm going to give some background information for those who are not familiar with this phrase.

Down through Christian history, there have been many reports of Our Lord Jesus Christ Himself appearing to people. There have also been reports of the Blessed Virgin Mary or other saints appearing to people. Except for Jesus and His Mother,[64] the bodies of all who have died, saints included, are in the grave. Sometimes these "apparitions," as they are called, were incredibly important because they saved people's lives. I'm reminded of one claimed apparition that no one has ever studied. It happened to a Franciscan brother I knew, a missionary in China, during World War II. The Japanese army was entering the city where he was. They could hear the machine guns, and so they all ran out the back gate of the city. He was with an old friar who could only go slowly up into the hills. At a certain juncture, they were going to turn right, but they saw

[64] Enoch (Gen. 5:22) and Elijah (2 Kings 2:11) departed this world bodily but without dying.

a man standing in their way. The man said, "No, go left!" and so they went left. Soon they heard the machine gun fire on the right. They say that brother was convinced that he had seen an angel.

What do you do with that? It saved his life. Who is it who gives these private revelations from the transcendent, mysterious world of eternity? They could be angelic creatures, heavenly citizens; or they could be apparitions of saints. The Church has had to deal with claims of this kind throughout Her history. I have considered private revelations in some depth, and I wrote a book about it, called *A Still Small Voice*.[65] Here's what we must say about this issue: the Church can never infallibly teach that a private revelation has taken place. Her infallible teachings are about the Scriptures and Tradition. The most the Church could do is give Her approval, and probably the strongest approval is given when a pope visits the place of the apparition—as, for example, Pope John Paul II's visits to Lourdes and to Fatima. Both were places where apparitions of Mary, the Mother of God, occurred: at Lourdes she visited St. Bernadette in 1858; at Fatima, she visited three little children, Lucía, Jacinta, and Francisco, in 1917. At Fatima, the children initially didn't know who they were talking to. Other people had to tell them that it was the Blessed Virgin. They reported what was told to them, much of which they didn't understand. For example, the children repeated the expression "Russia would be converted," but they thought that "Russia" was a person! They had no idea of geography.

Most private revelations reported and examined are not approved. Three revelations in modern times that have received the highest Church approval are the revelation to St. Margaret Mary Alacoque of the Sacred Heart of Jesus (1673–1675), the revelation

[65] San Francisco: Ignatius Press, 1993.

of Our Lady of the Immaculate Conception to St. Bernadette at Lourdes (1858), and the revelation of Divine Mercy to St. Maria Faustina (1931). In addition to these, there was a humble little nun named Catherine Labouré, to whom the Blessed Virgin gave the design of the Miraculous Medal (1830).

It's also important to know that even a saint who gives a report of a private revelation can make mistakes. Pope Benedict XIV wrote extensively on private revelations, noting that no such revelation is necessarily free from error, since, even if directly from God, it is filtered through the reporting of the person who received it.

Psychological Examinations for Priests and Religious

There seems to be a trend with religious orders and dioceses requiring psychological evaluations for candidates to the priesthood or the religious life. How does one choose a psychologist for this evaluation?

I was around when this all got started, and over the years, I have done about 2,500 evaluations of people wanting to study for the priesthood or the religious life. I may have the world record, and I assure you it's nothing to be jealous about because such testing is a long haul.

Why was it done? Not to figure out who was going to stay but to figure out who should try and who should not try. Through this examination process, I met some good people of goodwill who, because of their psychological profile, may have been very innocent and kindly people, but they had predictable things in their personalities that would make it very hard for them to live in a community and almost impossible for them to serve others in the role of pastor or priest. Not everybody is called to this. My patron saint, St. Benedict Joseph, was a Trappist eleven times! He never made it more than six weeks before he broke down every time and had to start over. I certainly would not have accepted him.

Purgatory: Is It Biblical?

Please explain what you know about Purgatory since it is not in the Bible. I am told that as Catholics, we see it as a place between Heaven and Hell.

It is true that the *word Purgatory* is not in the Bible. That word comes from St. Augustine in the fourth century. But the reality of Purgatory is found particularly in St. Paul. I would suggest a book of mine: *After This Life: What Catholics Believe about What Happens Next.*[66] It's about life, death, judgment, Hell, Purgatory, and Heaven. I should mention to you that Catholics, more than anybody else in the whole world, seem to know more about what happens after death, and over the centuries—over two thousand years—there has been a developing understanding of what happens.

To say that Purgatory is not in the Scriptures is not true. First of all, in the Old Testament, the Jewish people believed that after this life, there was another place before entering into eternal life, and that you could pray for those people. Particularly in the words of Maccabees, it is a holy and good thought to pray for the dead (2 Macc. 12:45). Jews to this day believe that, after this life, there is an interim before eternal life in which you can prepare yourself. Also, the Orthodox church believes that there is an interim between

[66] Huntington, IN: Our Sunday Visitor, 2009.

this life and eternal glory, though they don't use the word *Purgatory*. In their understanding, I am told, it's much like a journey, a road into eternal life, along which you do two things: you clarify, or perfect, your own soul, cleaning out things that are unworthy; and you pay the "tolls" for what you left behind you.

Now, Catholics believe the same thing, but in different words. We don't usually talk about it being a journey or a road, but there are the words of Our Lord, that "you will never get out till you've paid the last penny" (Matt. 5:26). There is a very interesting discussion about all this in an encyclical by Pope Benedict, *Spe Salvi*, "Saved in Hope." He writes very well about the idea of Purgatory, that you have to pay up what you have not paid up already. The pope writes about the early Jewish idea of an intermediate state, including the view that those souls are not simply in a sort of temporary custody, but as the parable of the rich man illustrates, they are being punished or experiencing a provisional form of blessing. There is also the idea that this state can involve purification and healing, which mature the soul for communion with God. The early Church took up these concepts, and in the Western Church—that is, people in the Latin world— the doctrine of Purgatory gradually developed.

We do not need to examine here the complex historical path of this development. It is enough to say what it actually means. At death, our life-choice becomes definitive; our life stands before our divine Judge. Our choice, over the course of an entire life, takes on a certain shape. Some have destroyed their desire for truth and readiness for love: these are people for whom everything has ever been a lie, who have lived for hatred and have suppressed all love within themselves. It's a terrifying thought. This is what we mean by *Hell*.

In life, we have a lot of experiences and choices, and sometimes we make compromises with evil. St. Paul, in his First Letter to the

Corinthians, gives us the idea that each person's particular circumstances have a different impact on God's judgment. He writes:

> Now if any one builds on the foundation with gold, silver, precious stones, wood, hay, stubble—each man's work will become manifest; for the Day will disclose it, because it will be revealed with fire, and the fire will test what sort of work each one has done. If the work which any man has built on the foundation survives, he will receive a reward. If any man's work is burned up, he will suffer loss, though he himself will be saved, but only as through fire. (3:12–15)

During the very early stages of the Church, from the beginning, people were praying for the dead, and whenever you pray for the dead, you're saying that there is something between Heaven and Hell, because people in those places don't need our prayers (Heaven), or they can't benefit from our prayers (Hell). It's a very sensible thing.

Now, because of the denial of Purgatory, Protestants generally believe that there is only Heaven or Hell. However, not very long ago, I went to the funeral of a very fine Protestant minister, a lifelong friend of mine. I was pleased to be invited to say a few words. At the end of the service, the minister who officiated led us all in a prayer that our friend would be on his journey to eternal life. I was amazed. But you know, it's a sensible idea. There was a great Protestant named Samuel Johnson, the editor of the first English dictionary and a great writer. If you studied English literature, you would remember Samuel Johnson. He was a High Church Anglican, and he believed in Purgatory. His secretary, Boswell, who was a Presbyterian, said, "Catholics believe in Purgatory." And Johnson said, "Why, Sir, it is a very harmless doctrine. They are of the opinion that the generality of mankind are neither so obstinately wicked as to deserve everlasting punishment, nor so good as to merit being admitted into the society of blessed spirits; and therefore that God is graciously pleased to allow a middle state, where they may be purified by certain degrees of suffering. You see, Sir, there is nothing unreasonable in this."[67]

Now, many people have their Purgatory in this life. That's an old Irish saying. Someone is terribly ill; terribly uncomfortable at the end of life. It used to be a saying that they had the Purgatory already. There's a lot of truth to that, because they held on to faith, to hope, to loving God, even though they were dying. That is a way to purify your heart and soul, so you can completely come to God. This does not mean that Jesus is not our Savior. He's our complete Savior, but in saving us, He gives us grace to do good. And that's part of salvation, doing good.

[67] Quoted in Karl Keating, "Purgatory," in *Catholicism and Fundamentalism* (San Francisco: Ignatius Press, 1988), EWTN, https://www.ewtn.com/catholicism/library/purgatory-982.

Purgatory: Is It a Metaphor?

You have spoken often about Purgatory, as though the soul needed to suffer in order to be made pure before entering Heaven. Scripture speaks of souls being purified by fire, but isn't this mostly metaphorical rather than real, since the soul is nonmaterial? The causal relation between suffering and penance for our sins seems to have no reasonable basis. Jesus suffered immeasurable pain and torments, but He in no way needed to do penance and be purified to enter Heaven. Also, the devil suffers eternal fire, but he in no way will be purified. How can these two examples comport with belief in a Purgatory of fire and suffering? Isn't the idea of the soul asleep more appropriate for those souls who do not merit direct entry into Heaven—namely, those of us who are not saints?

What is the relationship between the forgiveness of sins and suffering? And what about the suffering of fire after death? Obviously, the word *fire* applied after death cannot refer to physical fire, to oxidation, because the body is in the grave, decomposing or decomposed till the end of the world. St. Catherine of Genoa, the great mystic of Purgatory, says that it is the desire of the soul to come completely to the possession of God and to be united with God. That is, Purgatory is a fire of desire. This makes a lot of sense.

It's a mistaken notion to think that the pain and the fire take away our sins. Our sins are taken away only by the holy and precious blood of Jesus Christ. But it is true that suffering in this world purifies our souls. You may know this yourself from your own experience. Think of those times in life when you really matured, when you did better, grew more virtuous; when—if I can use a Jersey City expression—you "cleaned up your act." Many of these growth experiences were times of suffering. There are people here who didn't have any concern for God until someone dear to them died. There are people reading this who are now quite ill and, because of that, are very interested in what happens next after they die. They might never have thought about it if they had not become ill. So suffering is not superficially linked to maturity by any means. After all, when the Christian's soul is ready to enter the presence of God, it has matured.

Then the questioner asks whether the idea of the sleep of the soul is more appropriate for those souls who do not merit direct entry into Heaven. Cardinal Newman beautifully brings together the idea of penance and suffering and sleep and rest. But is divine justice not fulfilled by the experience of Purgatory? The Scriptures aren't terribly clear about it. As I've already noted above, Our Lord refers to it once, speaking of the man who will not get out of jail until he has paid the last penny (Matt. 5:26); and St. Paul, too, wrote about being purified by fire (1 Cor. 3:15). It seems to me that Purgatory is common sense.

I can't answer for you, but I know that I could be doing better, and I know one of the reasons I'm not doing better now is because I didn't do better in the past. It's a journey, and I've got a lot of steps that I haven't taken at the ripe old age of seventy-four. I'm looking forward to the future. If an angel appeared to me and said, "You can go straight to Heaven or go to Purgatory to tidy up your whole act," I would go to Purgatory because of the very thought of coming before the pure white radiance of God's infinite goodness in my present unseemly state, with my tendencies toward sin, impatience, and unkindness. I don't lead a sinful life, my Lord, but I don't by any means lead a perfect Christian life. If I could be more prepared to enter before the divine majesty, before our beloved Lord Jesus Christ, Who loves me so very much—I, who love Him half-heartedly—if I could open my soul completely to the Holy Spirit, then I would be at peace going into the Kingdom of Heaven. Don't worry, I absolutely believe that Christ saves us, that we do not save ourselves. But we can make ourselves ready to receive His infinite blessing.

Purgatory: St. Catherine of Genoa, St. John Henry Newman, and *Spe Salvi*

We received several questions about Purgatory. These questions are proposed both by the concern that people have for deceased relatives and by the teachings of Pope Benedict on Purgatory in his encyclical Spe Salvi, *"Saved in Hope." There is much interest in this question as people are concerned about their own future and about the welfare of their deceased relatives. What is the teaching of the Church and of Pope Benedict on Purgatory?*

Not very long ago, I assisted at a funeral in a Protestant church, and as I was leaving, the minister, a very kindly woman, said to me, "You know, I think you Catholics are absolutely right about Purgatory." I was rather surprised.

Paragraphs 44–46 of Pope Benedict's encyclical *Spe Salvi* is relevant to this question about Purgatory. In paragraph 45, the pope points out that the ancient Jewish people believed in an intermediate state in which souls were not simply in custody but were either being punished or experiencing a provisional form of happiness. The early Church then took up these concepts, and in the Western Church, they developed into the concept of Purgatory. This word, which means "cleansing," comes from St. Augustine, who wrote of "the cleansing fires of Purgatory." Unfortunately—and you know I love St. Augustine—if I had had a chance to talk to him, I would have said not to use the word *fire* because fire is a material phenomenon, and the soul is immaterial; the soul in Purgatory has no body. Therefore, the use of the word *fire* in association with Purgatory is symbolic because it's impossible to burn a soul. Despite the symbolism, people have found it rather terrifying.

The Holy Father follows St. Catherine of Genoa's idea of Purgatory. It's a very beautiful idea: she says that the happiness of the holy souls in Purgatory is exceeded only by the happiness of the souls in Heaven. Where, then, do we get this gruesome image of Purgatory as an annex of Hell, pitchforks and all? That comes from Dante, the Italian poet, who presented this gruesome picture in his *Divine Comedy*. Even Dante softened it up a bit, but in the nineteenth century, the whole thing got even more gruesome. Influential here is a book that I hate, called *Purgatory*, written over a century ago by Fr. F. X. Schouppe, S.J., and still in publication.[68] Fr. Schouppe's book is based on legends and on distortions of what the saints say, in particular the words of St. Catherine of Genoa. If ever I wanted to be pope, it would have been so that I could put this book on the Index of Forbidden Books.[69] But listen to St. Catherine of Genoa, who is the great mystic of Purgatory:

> The soul was created as well conditioned as it is capable of being for reaching perfection if it live as God has ordained and do not foul itself with any stain of sin. But having

[68] Charlotte, NC: Tan, 2012; originally published in English translation by Benziger Brothers in 1926. The Imprimatur of the original French edition was given in 1893.

[69] The Index was a list of books deemed, by a special Congregation of the Vatican, to be heretical or contrary to Catholic morals. It was abolished by Pope St. Paul VI in 1966.

fouled itself by original sin, it loses its gifts and graces and lies dead, nor can it rise again save by God's means. And when God, by baptism, has raised it from the dead, it is still prone to evil, inclining and being led to actual sin unless it resist. And thus it dies again.

Then God by another special grace raises it again, yet it stays so sullied and so turned to self that all the divine workings of which we have spoken are needed to recall it to its first state in which God created it; without them it could never get back thither. And when the soul finds itself on the road back to its first state, its need to be transformed in God kindles in it a fire so great that this is its Purgatory. Not that it can look upon this as Purgatory, but its instinct to God, aflame and thwarted, makes Purgatory.

A last act of love is done by God without help from man. So many hidden imperfections are in the soul that, did it see them, it would live in despair. But in the state of which we have spoken they are all burnt away, and only when they have gone does God shew them to the soul, so that it may see that divine working which kindles the fire of love in which its imperfections have been burnt away.[70]

St. Catherine also says this:

Know that what man deems perfection in himself is in God's sight faulty, for all the things a man does which he sees or feels or means or wills or remembers to have a perfect seeming are wholly fouled and sullied unless he acknowledge them to be from God. If a work is to be perfect it

70 *Treatise on Purgatory*, chap. 11, EWTN, https://www.ewtn.com/catholicism/library/treatise-on-purgatory-9820.

> must be wrought in us but not chiefly by us, for God's works must be done in Him and not wrought chiefly by man.
>
> Such works are those last wrought in us by God of His pure and clean love, by Him alone without merit of ours, and so penetrating are they and such fire do they kindle in the soul, that the body which wraps it seems to be consumed as in a furnace never to be quenched until death. It is true that love for God which fills the soul to overflowing, gives it, so I see it, a happiness beyond what can be told, but this happiness takes not one pang from the pain of the souls in Purgatory. Rather the love of these souls, finding itself hindered, causes their pain; and the more perfect is the love of which God has made them capable, the greater is their pain.
>
> So that the souls in Purgatory enjoy the greatest happiness and endure the greatest pain; the one does not hinder the other.[71]

So St. Catherine, and Pope Benedict in his encyclical, see the sufferings of the souls in Purgatory as part of their coming into contact with God. I would suggest that you read a book for which I wrote the introduction. It is a translation of Catherine of Genoa's writings by Dr. Serge Hughes called *Catherine of Genoa: Purgation and Purgatory, the Spiritual Dialogue*. Based on that incredible book—which, by the way, profoundly influenced many Protestants in the nineteenth century—Cardinal John Henry Newman wrote a fascinating poem called *The Dream of Gerontius*.[72] It was one of the most popular writings in England in the middle of the nine-

[71] *Treatise on Purgatory*, chap. 12.

[72] EWTN, https://www.ewtn.com/catholicism/library/dream-of-gerontius-4107.

teenth century. It is said of Lord Gordon that, when he was killed in battle at Khartoum, he had a copy of *The Dream of Gerontius* in his pocket. The great Cardinal Newman, in that classic poem, depicts the soul, which begins to suffer when it comes into the presence of Christ; yet it knows it must do this. It is an angel who gently puts the soul in the healing waters of Purgatory to be finally made ready to enter into eternal life.

Now, I know it sounds a bit scary, but it's not horrible. I could compare it to how I feel before I go to the hospital for an operation, and I've had lots of them. You don't want to do this, but at the same time you do want to do it because it makes you healthy. I'm hoping that, with the pope's encyclical, there's going to be an increased interest in what the state of the soul is after death and that people will be filled with hope. The pope says that through prayer we are united with the holy souls on their way. He says that none of us are here alone, quoting John Donne, saying that "no man is an island." We suffer with each other, we struggle with each other, and when someone is dead, we must reach out to them through our prayers, to help them on their journey.

So it is a very beautiful thing. In my old age, the faces of so many people from the past, even when I was a small child in the 1930s, come back to me. I don't know why people I hardly knew come to mind, or people who were at the edges of my life—my old caddy master, a guy who yelled at me for no reason. When those memories come back to me, I pray for them on their journey, and I ask God to spare them, to bring them to fulfillment. This gives us great hope.

Maybe the gruesome pictures of Purgatory borrowed from Dante will recede into the background because of the writings of Pope Benedict.

Purity: How to Cultivate It in the World

Maybe I am too pessimistic, but in our pagan society, it seems impossible to reach purity when we all participate directly or indirectly in evil each day. Unless we live the life of John the Baptist, we cannot do God's will in society. Can our personal conversion lead to anything but a life like John the Baptist's?

Even John the Baptist got involved in society, because when he preached to the Roman soldiers, he told them to be content with their pay. If you want to say that he didn't get involved, he should have told the soldiers to go back home to Greece, which is where the Roman soldiers in the Holy Land were from. He should have protested the military occupation of Judea; he should have been a complete pacifist, but he wasn't. This means that we've got to live in this world. God does not expect of us angelic purity. Because angels have no moving parts, they're not good models of human behavior; rather, they got one chance at the beginning of their existence, a pass-fail grade, so to speak: yes or no.

Unlike the angels, human beings struggle with human weakness and with the effects of that mysterious reality called Original Sin. What God expects of us is that we will do our best. If I ever met anyone who told me that they led a virtuous life, that they committed no sins, that they had no contact with evil in any way, I would run away from such a person. I would try to get to the car as quickly as possible and drive away because this person is dangerous. As it really happens in the genuine spiritual life, as a person makes more progress, they come to see where they are lacking in virtue, and they try to get a little bit more virtue in those areas. That's why it's very disconcerting to work with someone like Mother Teresa, which I did for years; or to know Venerable Fr. Solanus Casey, who is proposed for beatification;[73] or even my good friend Cardinal Terence Cooke, who was declared a Servant of God, the first step toward canonization. None of these people tried to make themselves exempt from all the problems of humanity. Cardinal Cooke absolutely loved to play baseball. Even in conversation, he used baseball analogies. Mother Teresa rode the bus, and in New York City, the buses contribute to air pollution. Mother Teresa could be very quietly and very sweetly difficult to handle. Once her mind was made up that this is what God wanted, get out of the way!

If you read the New Testament, you'll see that the Apostles committed big sins and had big failures. You might say that, in one sense, the worst thing that ever happened to Peter was that he met Jesus, because he *was* going to betray Him. I imagine Peter might have said, "Look, I betrayed the Son of God." But that never would have happened to him if he had remained a fisherman.

I think our questioner is involved in what is called obsessive-compulsive thinking. You're very sincere; you're trying very hard; but you need to put yourself in the hands of God and trust Him. I recommend to you a book, one of the great classics of the spiritual life, called *Abandonment to Divine Providence*, by Jean-Pierre de Caussade. This is a marvelous book that will teach you how to let God lead you along.

[73] Blessed Fr. Solanus Casey was beatified on November 18, 2017.

Religions: Christian and Non-Christian

In the last several months, Pope Benedict has been in touch, not only with many Christian leaders, including the Orthodox patriarchs, but also with quite a few non-Christian leaders and denominations. When I grew up, I understood that the Catholic Church was the unique true Church of Christ. Why should we be involved with these other religions and denominations?

The very simple answer is because the people involved in those religions or denominations have immortal souls. God loves them; He is not a Catholic, nor is He Orthodox: God is God. Catholics certainly do believe that this is the true Church founded by Christ, sent through history to bring to the world the sacraments, the true teaching of Christ, and the tradition of the Apostles. But do the Catholics make terrible mistakes? They certainly do, and in that respect, we're no better than anybody else. In fact, we might be a lot worse, because if you really believe that you're the true Church, you'd better start acting that way, and Catholics sometimes don't.

The present Holy Father and the previous popes opened the doors to the other Christians and the other major religions of the world because we are all children of God, and we are all called to follow the divine law. The Church has always believed that the natural law is written on the hearts of everyone: not to kill, not to steal, not to lie, not to blaspheme, et cetera.

These are the things that bring us together. It was extremely interesting that, in his recent visit to New York, Pope Benedict met in one place the Catholic, Protestant, and Orthodox leaders. Then he had a separate meeting with non-Christian believers: Jews, Muslims, Buddists, Hindus, Jains. There were quite a few of them. The pope used a word that I have never heard a pope use in that context—a very simple, first-person plural pronoun: *we*. The pope said several times that "we" must work together to see that God's law is received in the world; that "we" must teach people to observe the divine law; and that "we" must work together for human dignity. I had never heard that before. I never could have imagined a pope calling the religions of the world "we." Now, does anybody think that Pope Benedict is not a Catholic, that he doesn't believe the Catholic Church is the true religion? Of course not. But he is looking at things with a different emphasis. And this is very important.

Years ago, I was in Hong Kong, and I wanted to go up and visit the big Buddhist shrine. Two Maryknoll sisters were with me, wearing the habit, and the three of us walked up many hundreds of steps. It was getting hot, and coming down the steps was a very old Buddhist monk, in a black robe, with a little umbrella to keep the sun off him. We bowed to each other, and when he bowed, he looked at me and touched his heart and then reached out and touched my heart. I thought that was a very beautiful sign. I could not imagine that God would ever disapprove of that. Thanks be to God that the religions of the world are largely talking to each other. They may be arguing, but they're showing the respect that we should show to any child of God.

Religious Orders

My wife and I are United Methodists, and we very much enjoy your Sunday Night Live *program. My question is on Catholic orders. We hear that someone is "a Dominican" or "a Jesuit" or "a Franciscan." We see the different initials for the orders, which we do not really understand. Can you explain the nature of the religious communities and how they differ?*

What the questioner is referring to is not the same as different denominations. The difference between a Methodist, a Baptist, and a Presbyterian is not the difference between a Dominican, Franciscan, or Jesuit, who are all Catholics, and all Catholics are under the pope. The major superiors of all religious orders are either, for the smaller orders, under a bishop, or, for the larger ones, under the pope. Our little community, the Franciscan Friars of the Renewal, is about twenty years old, but it has grown very quickly, and it is about to become what they call a "pontifical order," directly under the pope. Up until this time, we have been under our local bishop, the archbishop of New York.

Each one of these groups, or orders, has its own customs and ways, which reveal its particular Catholic spirituality. We have missionary orders such as the Maryknolls. In that order, everyone hopes to be a foreign missionary. Many religious communities work very hard at apostolic works. For example, the Jesuits, the

Franciscans, and the Dominicans work in society directly with ordinary people. But these orders work in different ways. Jesuits often are educators, as are the Dominicans. Our community exists to care for the very poor, the homeless, those who don't have enough to eat. Although I happen to be a teacher, the work of our community and its spiritual traditions define us as a religious order. Then there are the Trappists, monks who live a quiet, silent life of prayer and work, supporting themselves by manual labor, producing cheese or bread or various other things. Trappists present a totally different kind of experience. But that's why you have different religious communities: they offer a variety of Catholic spiritualities that serve to enrich the life of the Church.

The Franciscans were inspired by St. Francis; the Dominicans, by St. Dominic. St. Ignatius is the ideal of the Jesuits. Most of the old orders were founded by a single saint or perhaps several saints together. If you read their books, you'll find that they rejoice in what their "specialty" is.

The Resurrection: Did Jesus Visit His Mother?

Did Jesus see His Holy Mother between the Resurrection and the Ascension?

Nothing in Scripture indicates that He did. However, the Franciscan Order, being largely made up of emotional slobs, long ago concluded that Christ indeed appeared to His Mother after the Resurrection and before He ascended into Heaven. We Franciscans have the seven-decade Crown Rosary, which I have on, of which one of the mysteries is the apparition of Christ to Mary after the Resurrection.

There is a very good argument for this. Would any good son, especially a good Jewish boy, not go to see his mother after he came back from the dead? Probably many people watching this program have seen a carved relief statue of the apparition at the Church of the Holy Sepulchre. If you've ever gone to the Holy Land and visited the Holy Sepulchre, you know that, right inside the great dome, the Catholics have a chapel run by the Franciscans. On the front of the altar is a carved relief figure of Christ, with many halos showing supernatural glory, standing in front of the figure of a woman kneeling in profound adoration. At first, I thought it was Mary Magdalene, but I found out later that it was the Chapel of the Apparition, of Christ's appearing to His Mother, Mary, after the Resurrection. You can accept it as a devout opinion. It goes back a long way.

Returning to the Church

I am a lapsed Catholic. It has been some thirty years since I've participated in Church life and received the sacraments. I have nevertheless always continued to think of myself as Catholic and have always expected to pick up where I left off – but never have. I find it difficult to find my way back to the Church. I've tried attending Mass a few times, but I feel like a Catholic fish out of water. I've forgotten the prayers and how to follow along with the Mass, and I am embarrassed and overwhelmed to go back to Confession, thirty years after my last one. I hunger to receive the sacrament of Penance, to receive Communion, to have a prayer life, and to live my life in a Christ-centered way. How does a lapsed Catholic like me reenter the lifestyle of the Church, and where do I start?

That's an excellent question, and I should say that priests are delighted to help people who have been out of the Church a while. The friars and I hear confessions in St. Patrick's Cathedral[74] on Fridays. And people will come in and say, "Oh, Father, I haven't been to confession in eight years." I say, "Wonderful! It makes my trip here worthwhile today, and if I get a parking ticket, it will be worth it." Now, seriously, priests, deacons, other people who help

[74] In New York City.

in parishes—we're all delighted to have somebody come back, and I think you'll only find a warm welcome.

What you really need is a friend. Given your feelings of being overwhelmed by the thought of returning to an authentic Catholic life, you need someone among your friends who is a good Catholic, who will go with you to Mass, perhaps arranging for you to go to Confession and to rejoice with you, and maybe have a little celebration when you receive the sacraments for the first time. It would also be helpful if you made an appointment to go to Confession rather than going in the confessional. We're perfectly happy to hear in the confessional people who have been away for thirty years, but you might feel more comfortable if you could sit down with a priest and talk to him. Of course, maybe you'd rather it be anonymous. In either case, ask around for a priest who is known as a kindly confessor. Some priests have wonderful reputations for hearing confession gently and kindly. Make it easier for yourself; make it a human experience. Don't think of it in a mechanical way. It should be enjoyed. The Church is not a machine. It's a human experience.

Satan: Should We Hate Him?

Is it a sin to hate Satan? A friend of mine said God does not hate Satan, so we should not hate Satan but should pray that God will deliver us from temptations. Is this true or not?

I think your friend is out on thin ice. In part, the question is, what do you mean by "hate"? If you mean an angry mood, an unjust resentment, then of course God doesn't have that. God doesn't have moods. Does God totally and absolutely reject evil? Utterly. And we know from Scripture that there are these other intelligent beings different from human beings, beings of another domain of being, of a world that is not physical, a world that it is very difficult for us to even imagine, a world of persons: some dedicated to goodness, called angels, others utterly turned evil, called devils. These latter are very far from God because they have made a final decision, as have those human beings who are in eternal Hell. If you want to say that God "hates" them, you would have to do a lot of explaining of that. But certainly they are, by their own choice, cut off from God. No one can be lost who has not looked into the eyes of God and said, "I will not serve." That's important to keep in mind.

Scripture and Speculation

Just before Christmas, British Sky television put out a short program about Bethlehem and the birth of Our Lord. The presenter introduced an Israeli archaeologist who claimed that Jesus was not born in Bethlehem of Judea but, rather, in Bethlehem of Galilee. Is this just another conspiracy theory about Our Lord's birth, or is there any validity to the claim?

I'm answering this question not because of the discussion of Bethlehem of Judea versus Bethlehem of Galilee—which I never heard of—but because the questioner invoked the idea of conspiracy. Though there are, of course, conspiracies, it's not a good idea to see a lot of things in life as conspiracies.

Real conspiracies are usually very subtle, and people don't even realize they're going on. But this case focuses on the person of Jesus and on the reliability of the Gospels. I would say it's not a conspiracy, but it is a detectable movement to belittle the truth of the Gospels. Pope Benedict speaks about this very effectively in the preface to his book *Jesus of Nazareth*,[75] which I highly recommend.

[75] *Jesus of Nazareth* is a three-volume series: *From the Baptism in the Jordan to the Transfiguration* (New York: Doubleday, 2007); *Holy Week: From the Entrance into Jerusalem to the Resurrection* (San Francisco: Ignatius, 2011); and *The Infancy Narratives* (New York: Image, 2012).

There has been a constant trend since the nineteenth century to call the Gospels into question on supposedly scientific grounds. I'm glad that I didn't study Scripture; I studied science, and I wrote a *scientific* dissertation for my doctorate. Because of my scientific training, I realize that what they're talking about is not scientific at all. One of the first rules of science—perhaps *the* first rule—is: never try to prove a negative hypothesis. Never try to prove that something never happened.

No one can prove that they never committed a murder. You can't prove that. Somebody would have had to follow you with a television camera twenty-four hours a day for your whole life to prove that you never committed a murder. Biblical scholars often say that Jesus didn't do this, or that He didn't say that, or that He was born in another place. Why do they make these unscientific claims? Why is there this trend to belittle the life of Jesus, when there is no person from the ancient world whose public life is better known, more studied or evaluated. There is no other ancient life that comes near it. Nobody's ever even studied George Washington that way. Or Abraham Lincoln. Despite all the scholarship on them, neither of them has been studied as they've studied Christ. Why call the Gospels into question? The answer is simple: because Christ makes demands on you, and not just from the past, like a philosopher or a saint.

St. Francis tells you to be a peaceful, kindly person and to treat animals well. He says that from the past, and we hear it in his writings. Jesus, on the other hand, is here with us: "I am with you to the end of the age" (see Matt. 28:20). There are millions of people who believe that Christ Jesus of Nazareth is not only still alive but is near to them. There are also other people who don't believe at all, or don't believe very much, yet who understand what Christians believe, and it makes them uncomfortable; it gives them the jitters. How can Jesus, who died two thousand years ago, be with us now? I remember on the radio many years ago, an interviewer said to Mother Teresa, "Mother Teresa, what's your view on abortion?" She answered him, "What do you think Jesus thinks about abortion?" He was utterly speechless. He had never spent a minute thinking about what Jesus thought about anything or whether Jesus was still thinking about things. Mother Teresa's question was very threatening. As a matter of fact, though the interviewer was apparently an unbeliever, his wife, a few weeks later, joined the Missionaries of Charity volunteers. She was happy that somebody put a shell through his blimp.

Why does Jesus make people uncomfortable? Because He is here, and He expects us to obey His commandments and to live according to the precepts of the Sermon on the Mount. I assume that most of the people reading this believe all this about Jesus. It is what brings Christians together, and consequently, we must be prepared for people to be uncomfortable with that, for people to try to tear it down. I'm sorry to say that this very desire to tear down is prevalent in religious higher education, in colleges and universities that call themselves by Christian names. This is not the case with everybody, but it is true of many, and that's why I, along with the pope and the Cardinal Newman Society, have taken a very strong stand that Catholic schools must be genuinely Christian schools and that they must not tear down who Jesus Christ is but must, in all that they do, build up our appreciation, our awareness, our docility, and our willingness to accept Jesus Christ as the Way, the Truth, and the Life.

Service and Suffering

The practice of service to others is a foundation block of who I am. I believe that we were put on this earth to serve God *and one another. I practice it faithfully as a wife and mother. However, something seems to change when you attempt to serve in the real world. Manipulation and exploitation – that's what seems to happen. Ultimately, it manifests itself as resentment. I find that the biggest offenders are the ones who don't really need anything but just want to take advantage, and that stings. How can one discern the difference between giving glory to* God *in service and becoming a convenient doormat?*

It's a great question. The friars and sisters that I belong to take care of the poor and the homeless, and I have been very involved with the poor all my life as a priest. I took the name Benedict Joseph because my patron saint was a homeless, mentally ill man: St. Benedict Joseph Labre.

Now, I love to take care of the poor. First, it's a great deal of fun. If you've never taken care of the poor directly, let me tell you, you've missed one of the most interesting parts of life. The poor are not afraid to be their real selves. They're not always enjoyable, but they're always real.

Secondly, there is all the phony poor. I figure that, over the years, probably 10 to 12 percent of the poor to whom I gave material support didn't really deserve it. Some of these undeserving recipients thought that they did deserve it; they thought they were poorer than they actually were. Others weren't trying to support themselves, and so they were bending the truth a little bit. The bad ones, the true crooks, took maybe 5 percent of the goods. Do you realize what a wonderful country this would be if all the people who charge us taxes were only ripping us off 5 percent? My goodness, if they were only ripping us off 12 percent, the whole United States would be a very different place! And many of these officials don't need to rip people off, but that's how life goes.

They say there are three ways to do anything: the inexpensive way, the expensive way, and the government way. Get the government to do it, and they will spend a whole lot more money than anybody else would have spent doing the same thing. We've run a home for boys. I started working there in 1968. Many hundreds of young men have gone on from there, many of them now forty or fifty years old, with careers of varying degrees of success. I ran that home for them, and it never cost the government a nickel. The boys themselves pitched in and earned part of their keep. Now, if we had gotten a lot of government aid, we would have wasted money. Sorry to tell you, though, many projects can't exist without government aid. They would never get started.

I know what it means to get ripped off while trying to help the poor, but remember: Jesus doesn't say, "I was hungry and you gave me something to eat, except when you were afraid of getting ripped off." Last year, a friend of mine, Bishop Robert Baker, published a book called *When Did We See You, Lord?*[76] It has beautiful meditations on the Gospel of giving away. One of the things that Mother Teresa often said to me, speaking about people who took

[76] Huntington, IN: Our Sunday Visitor Press, 2005.

advantage of her or criticized her, was this: "It's not between me and them. It's between me and God, and them and God." So if you're giving away out of the love of God, don't be too worried about whether you're being taken advantage of. You must watch and be careful, of course, but it's between you and God. I certainly would rather make the mistake of giving to a person who doesn't need it than to deny a person who has great personal needs. Look around in society, and you'll see that there are all sorts of wonderful things that are part of our society that came to be through the voluntary actions of generous people: for example, schools and universities were started by monks; hospitals were started by members of religious orders, especially friars. These places were started by people who wanted to do good. Cultivate the desire to do good, and you will find that your life will be filled with sunlight.

Sin against the Holy Spirit

What constitutes a sin against the Holy Spirit? Is this the sin that cannot be forgiven?

Our Lord says that all the blasphemies by which people blaspheme against God can be forgiven except to blaspheme against the Holy Spirit (Matt. 12:31–32). Now, what does the Holy Spirit do? He gives us the grace, the impulse, the knowledge, and the enlightenment to do the works of salvation. Christ has saved us, but it is the Holy Spirit who unites us with that salvation. To sin against the Holy Spirit, then, it would seem, is to reject that possibility of salvation. Pope John Paul II did address this question: in the last act of life, the Holy Spirit is still calling to the person, so if they reject Him, they know without a doubt that they're rejecting Goodness and Holiness. They have chosen everlasting death. It's an appalling thought. We who are believers should pray that no one will go against the Holy Spirit. I have friends who have lost their faith. Some consider themselves atheists, but I have prayed for them every day, that the Holy Spirit will come to them and that they will accept Him.

Have you heard about the agnostic who went to Mass every Sunday? Somebody asked him why he goes to Mass every Sunday if he's an agnostic. "It might be true," he answered.

What are you going to do if it's true?

Sin: Speaking Clearly about It

When I was growing up, there was often a discussion about sin. Now you hardly ever hear anyone mention mortal or venial sin. Are those things that were sins in the past no longer a moral problem? I am confused.

You're very right to be confused. We do not speak clearly about sin, and consequently, we are in a situation in the United States—our whole culture—where the vast majority, even those who believe, are lulled into dullness about sin. I think it's right to tell people about sin and to encourage them to avoid it. Sometimes people talk about sin in such an angry way that it doesn't do any good. But I totally agree with you: we should identify it.

Suicide

We received several inquiries about suicide and how responsible people are when they take their own lives and what the outcome of suicide is. Simply put, are those who commit suicide lost? We talked about this already, but it seems to me that we need to discuss it a bit more, because so many people seem to be concerned about it.

Recently on one of our broadcasts, a very good-sounding, heartbroken man mentioned that his dear wife, in depression, had taken her own life just a few weeks before. You wouldn't be a clergyman very long before you would have to attend to such a situation. Priests, ministers, and rabbis are familiar with a situation where a perfectly good person struggling to deal with life is hit with a deep depression, what somebody has described as a "black tornado," and they take their own life.

Sometimes they do it in a minute and a half. One minute, they're sitting in a room chatting, and the next, they go upstairs and take their life. You might ask: How in the world did this happen? Religion has concluded that most people who do this are not in their right mind. To take your own life in your right mind would be a serious sin against God. It would be a violation of the commandment "Thou shalt not kill." Out of the Middle Ages and up into modern times came the discipline of denying Christian burial to people who committed suicide.

All my life as a priest, however, I knew that people who had committed suicide had a priest praying at the funeral parlor for them, trying to console the family and to bring hope to them, and now I'm happy to say that we make the presumption that for a person to do something so terrible to themselves, they must not be thinking clearly. That may not be true in all cases of suicide, but it seems to me that it is true in most. Some people can't handle the pain of life anymore, and others have a temporary insanity come upon them. These are different kinds of suicide, and every one of us must have compassion and must pray that these people are saved. In the cases I have been involved with, it was quite clear that the people were not in control of themselves. Some of the people reading this, trying to understand this, may recall that at some very difficult time in life, they said, "I wish I were dead." That can be a suicidal remark.

Let's put everybody who comes to this dark end of the road, through mental illness, through extreme depression, lovingly in the hands of God. And let's remember the words of Jesus: "I did not come to judge the world, but to save the world" (John 12:47). Let's remember that, in every Mass, Catholics say, "Lamb of God, who takes away the sins of the world, have mercy on us."

Theodicy: God's Justice and Human Suffering

I have always been a person of faith and have trusted in God. I am not losing my faith, but I'm very disappointed and feel abandoned by Him. I have a twenty-year-old daughter who was having a difficult time with life and has psychological problems. Although she is under treatment by a psychiatrist, she is lonely and can't seem to form healthy friendships with her peers. I have prayed and prayed for her that God will bring good people into her life, I have encouraged my daughter to pray as well. Does God punish us for our sins by allowing these things to happen in our family? I have even tried to make amends with God by going to Confession.

Let me say this to you: you're placing on yourself the responsibility for your daughter's misfortune. Your daughter obviously has some psychological difficulties, and they are infringing on her young life. You're doing the best you can by getting her psychiatric treatment. Perhaps behind this, you're struggling with the idea that you may have caused your daughter's problems, perhaps by some mistakes or things you did in the past. There's no question that we do affect other people's psychological adjustment: our children, people we meet on the way through life. A total stranger may intrude on a person's life and, by abusing them, upset their adjustment. It is necessary to live in the present moment and also to look back and see what mistakes you might have made. But you cannot undo the past; you can only work in the present.

As for the idea that God is visiting a punishment on your daughter because of you, that's a very primitive religious idea. It doesn't fit into Christianity at all. You'll find echoes of that kind of thinking in the Old Testament, where many of the ideas have been supplanted by New Testament thinking. You're never going to find that in the teachings of Our Lord. What you must do is patiently meet your daughter where she is in her struggle, encourage her, and stick by her. Always be there for her with a friendly smile. Do things with her; take her out to places and events. Get involved with her care, and talk to the psychiatrist about ways you could assist integrating her into the larger community.

She may need to belong to one of those twelve-step groups that I mentioned with the previous question on depression.[77] Perhaps in your area there is an anonymous twelve-step group that's for recovery or for people who are troubled. Maybe your daughter's psychiatrist could help her to get involved in one of those groups. Also, doing things for other people is immensely helpful. The best way to get out of the prison of your own self is to be involved hands-on in the needs of other people. Being a psychologist and spiritual director, I can look at myself and ask what in the world I would have been like if I had not had the impulse to help other people!

Mental health is not something that you just carry through life, like a badge; it's something that we all work on and all of us could fail if we stop working on it. This is a challenge to you. It's not helpful to think that God has done this as a punishment.

[77] See "Depression," above.

Thomas à Kempis's Death

I recently bought The Imitation of Christ, *written by Thomas à Kempis (1380–1471). I think this is a book all sincere Catholics should read. Thomas à Kempis was a mystic of the Catholic Church who died when he was accidentally buried alive. Splinters were found underneath his fingernails. He was not canonized because "a saint would not fight death in this way." My question is: Isn't it a normal human reaction to do what Thomas did? If Thomas had just lain there and died, wouldn't that be a form of suicide?*

The interesting case of Thomas à Kempis can be put this way. Nobody ever formally declared that he couldn't be canonized. They did not present his cause for beatification because of the possibility that he died in despair, not because he struggled to get out of the casket. I think any normal person finding themselves in such a situation would certainly make such an attempt, and it was not totally unknown for people to be accidentally buried alive before the advent of the procedures that we now have, like embalming. You can't get buried alive if you're embalmed. So when Thomas's body was exhumed as part of the process of beatification, they discovered this terrible and unfortunate fact.

Now, an important part of the process of beatification is an evaluation of the last hours and minutes, the last attitudes and prayerfulness, and the conscious attitudes of the person who is dying. That's an important part of the procedure, and in Thomas's case, there is no way to know it. Since I am a fan of Thomas à Kempis, I think it almost certain that he understood this terrible reality and he accepted it. Certainly, he tried to get out; but if you think of it, maybe when we get to the eternal Kingdom of God, we'll find that Thomas à Kempis is there with the marytrs, who endured terrible things. I wouldn't think any the less of him.

It is, I think, something you should know, though, that quite a few serious scholars think that He did not write all four books of *The Imitation of Christ*. They're written in rather different styles, and there may be other authors, such as Gerard Groote, who worked on it. It's interesting to study about.

Translation of Prayers

At the end of the Glory Be, we say, "world without end. Amen." This statement is contrary to a major theme of the New Testament, which is the end of the world and the final judgment. Is this prayer a bad translation? If so, why doesn't it get corrected?

I wouldn't say that it's a bad translation, but it is an awkward translation. What it says in Latin is *per omnia saecula saeculorum*, "throughout all the ages of ages." The Latin word *saecula* means "age." In this context, it is really referring to eternity, "the ages of ages." The problem in the translation quoted is the use of the English word *world*. We typically think of *world* as the earth, the solar system, the material universe, but that's not all it means. There are other meanings. For example, we might say that something comes from "the world," and we mean by that from "the seemingly stupid segment of society that's totally given over to materialistic things," and we say that such a thing is "worldly."

On the other hand, Jesus speaks of "the world to come," referring to eternal life. So, you can use *world* or the Latin word *saecula* to speak either of this creation or of the eternal creation. That latter reference would be the "world without end." While it's not such a good translation, it doesn't contradict the New Testament.

There is a translation of another word that slightly drives me crazy, and I'm willing to collect money to get them to change this one. In the Creed we say, "He descended into hell." He did not. What it says in Latin is *descendit ad inferos. Inferos* does not mean "Hell"; it means "the lower world," or "the lower regions" and is, in fact, what was called by the Fathers of the Church "limbo." This was the place where the Old Testament faithful waited for Christ to come and save the world, and it is called "the limbo of the Fathers." Jesus went there and announced the salvation of the world and called all the good people who had lived from Adam and Eve up until His time, including St. Joseph, into the eternal kingdom of eternal life. Some modern theologians, particularly one quite brilliant, Hans Urs von Balthasar, seem to suggest that Christ went into something like the eternal Hell, the Hell of the fallen angels, the Hell of those who are condemned, and that He suffered there. And the theological reason for saying this is because He wanted to redeem human beings from the worst. It's a new idea, and I must admit that it makes me uncomfortable for theological reasons. But it is a bad translation. We should say, "He descended into the lower world." Most people in modern times don't think that when Christ died, He went into anything like Hell. But we are left there with that translation.

There are many things that could be translated a little better. The problem is that language changes and words take on new meanings, and so you'd always be changing things. I suppose those in authority decided not to keep changing things, or we might get ourselves into some linguistic difficulties.

Tridentine Mass

Kindly comment on the following article[78] *about the Tridentine Mass.*

It is quite an article on the AT&T website for January 3, 2008, about Pope Benedict's liberalization of the rules of the old Latin Mass. This Mass is called by many people the Tridentine Mass. I said this Mass for four years because I was ordained in 1959, and I knew it quite well. I'm trying to relearn it in my old age. Unfortunately, with my broken arm, I can't make all the gestures that the Mass requires, but some of our friars are learning it, and I've been attending some Tridentine Masses to see if I can wake up my memory.

Now, the Holy Father put out a directive that all priests could offer the Mass without their bishop's approval if a "stable" group of parishioners requested it. Apparently, though, there have been some attempts in some dioceses—I don't know where—by various

[78] The AT&T website as of the time of publication of this book no longer curates news. However, it is quite possible that the following January 3, 2008, *USA Today* article is the one curated by AT&T and thus referenced by the questioner: Nicole Winfield, "Vatican to Elaborate on Pope's Liberalization of the Old Latin Mass," https://www.usatoday.com/story/news/nation-world/2008/01/04/vatican-to-elaborate-on-pope/52687643007/.

means to annul that decree of the pope, according to Msgr. Albert Malcolm Ranjith, secretary of the Congregation of Divine Worship.[79] This is wrong. Cardinal Bertone has said that some have even gone so far as to accuse the pope of having reneged on the Second Vatican Council's teachings. On the other side are those who have interpreted this document as authorization to return exclusively to the pre-Council rite. Both positions are wrong and are exaggerated opinions that don't correspond to the pope's intention.

The Holy Father has been very clear, as was Pope John Paul II, that any priest is permitted to say Mass in the vernacular according to the Novus Ordo, the new rite. Now, some are saying that any priest can offer the Mass in the old rite. There are people at each end of the spectrum trying to forbid people to do the opposite extreme. I think that's most unfortunate, and that is a tear in the unity of the Church. Those who support the Latin, or Tridentine, Rite do so because they believe that it will return a greater sense of reverence and awe to the Eucharist. And it is true that when the Tridentine Mass is said, it often does have great reverence and awe. But it didn't always. When I was a young priest, I decided that I would say Mass in Latin. And I got into trouble because I was too slow. I said every word as you're supposed to say it; I did not mumble it. It took up to four minutes longer, and some were annoyed, so the vernacular came in as an attempt to make the Mass more reverent and awesome. That was the purpose. Unfortunately, though, in the '70s and '80s, we adopted a very casual form of Christianity, which I think is decadent and intellectually inferior

[79] The full name was Congregation for Divine Worship and Discipline of the Sacraments. It is now called the *Dicastery* for Divine Worship and Discipline of the Sacraments.

and by no means a tribute to the Catholic Faith. I have been to liturgies where I was tempted to walk out.

I do have my own axe to grind. There are many liturgies in the Catholic Church, some of them far more ancient than the Roman liturgy that we use. There are the Syro-Malabar and Syro-Malankara Rites in India, which presumably go back to the time of St. Thomas. There's the liturgy of St. James, which is used, for instance, in the Armenian Catholic and Orthodox churches. There's the liturgy of St. John Chrysostom, archbishop of Constantinople, which most of us are familiar with as the Byzantine or Eastern Rite—Ukrainian, Ruthenian, Melkite, and other Eastern rites. There's also the Maronite Rite. There are many rites, and in all of them, the central part of the Mass, the Canon, is recited out loud. It was recited out loud in the Roman Canon up until about the twelfth century, when people no longer spoke Latin, but they did speak its daughter languages, such as Italian, French, and Spanish. It was then that the priests began the practice of *not* saying the Canon out loud. I think that was an abuse, and I would happily work the rest of my life to have the Canon said out loud so that people are participating fully in the life of the Church and the re-presentation of the Eucharistic sacrifice of Christ, which He began at the Last Supper.

The battles that can ensue are interesting, however; and they are sad because these battles are waged in the name of God and the name of Christ, Who, in contrast, says, "Peace be to you." *Peace.* It's unfortunate that throughout history, not only of the Church and of Christianity but of all the world religions, you can find people fighting about the way to do things. This is a sad commentary on religion, which the atheistic writers love to applaud.

I don't know whether the atheists themselves get along with each other very well. I've never been to a meeting of atheists.

Unbelief and Church Membership

I am a fallen-away cradle Catholic. I have been feeling a strong desire to return to the Church, mostly by watching EWTN, but I am struggling. After examination, I realize my big obstacle is the divinity of Jesus Christ. If I don't believe in the basics, why would I want to come back? And yet I feel so pulled to the Church and think this would help my unbelief. It is a vicious circle for me. I have always felt the real presence of God in my life, I try to live a good life, and I pray for the grace to believe.

Well, let me say that you're certainly doing the right thing to pray for the gift of faith, because faith *is* a gift. Unfortunately, at times, we Christians, in our zeal to get people to accept Christ as Savior, tend to forget that faith is a gift, a call that has to be responded to. You have this experience of being drawn toward Christianity, toward a particular church: that's a grace; but you don't seem to have the total grace to accept the absolute mystery of Christ.

Now, there are all kinds of people who will try to prove to you that Christ is the Son of God, and you should listen to them because those arguments [whether correct or not] are purportedly based on Scripture. They will tell you things that you likely don't realize or know about Christianity. But even if they talk you into Christianity, there is a high degree of probability that you won't stay. I've personally seen people who, talked into

Catholicism or into one of the Orthodox churches, stayed for a while but then left.

Just recently, the Evangelical publication *Christianity Today* gave an account of a biblical scholar who was apparently quite seriously convicted of faith in Christ and then lost it. According to this account, his attention was very much drawn to the words of Sacred Scripture, and when he discovered that what he was reading are translations—not always very accurate—of the Greek and Hebrew texts of Scripture, he apparently lost his faith completely. As I was reading the article, I thought how sad it was that one of two things happened: either he had faith and lost it, which can be done; or he had an experience of the virtue of religion, which is a natural virtue, but it never really became genuine faith.

Now, how can you recognize faith? Faith is a relationship of trust between two people, in this case, between human beings and God. If I were to have doubts about faith, I would see them as doubts about my best friend, about the person I value and esteem more than all other things put together, and I would struggle with those doubts and fight with them, and I would learn from them to try to help other people with doubt. This is what Cardinal Ratzinger [now Pope Emeritus Benedict XVI] suggests in his book *Introduction to Christianity*. Europe is instilled with doubt, he says, so let's confront it. From doubt we can move to faith, because doubt will bring us to our knees, to say to God: show me Your way.

If you really want to read about faith in Christ, read the whole Gospel of John, especially John 6 and then John 12 on to the end of the book. For example, in John 14, Jesus has just told His disciples that He is the Way, the Truth, and the Life. The way to God. The way to eternity. And Philip says, "Lord, show us the Father, and we shall be satisfied." And Jesus says to Philip,

> Have I been with you so long, and yet you do not know me, Philip? He who has seen me has seen the Father; how can you say, "Show us the Father"? Do you not believe that I am in the Father and the Father in me? The words that I say to you I do not speak on my own authority; but the Father who dwells in me does his works. Believe me that I am in the Father and the Father in me; or else believe me for the sake of the works themselves. (vv. 8–11)

This question from a fallen-away Catholic woman who wants to come back to church but does not accept that Christ is divine is an honest one, and she should be commended. There have been many people in the Church who pretend to accept Christ as the Lord, the only-begotten Son of God, but who really don't believe it. Our questioner is in much better shape than those who pretend to believe. In effect, she is saying, as so many have said, "Lord, help my unbelief" (see Mark 9:24). I would tell her to read especially, in addition to the writings of the New Testament, the writings of St. Augustine and St. Bonaventure, both Doctors of the Church, and the latter the eighth general of the Franciscan Order. The present pope[80] also: he is a disciple of both Augustine and Bonaventure.

Now, what happens when you do believe: Can you lose it? Obviously, some people are negligent with the Faith: they trade it for stupid things, they become worldly; they become intrigued by ideas untouched by faith. I work with real people who have very real problems, problems that could bring you to Heaven or to Hell. This last week, I had to bury a man I knew as a little boy. He had a terribly difficult childhood, and it showed up in his later life, and eventually he took his own life. I had to talk to his wife,

[80] Pope Benedict XVI.

his sons, his family. I told them that Christ was there with them, and all they had to do was to look for Him, and He can be found.

If you don't know about the Son of God, then you must read the Gospel with an open heart and mind and say, "Now, help my unbelief!" and He will help you. That would be far more impressive to me than the many arguments for Jesus' divinity, even arguments drawn from Scripture. The devil can quote the Bible if he wants to (e.g., Matt. 4:6). You should rather pray, saying, "Come, Lord Jesus!" and He will come. I'm a psychologist, and therefore I'm aware that people can suggest things for themselves and manufacture things out of their minds. But God is real: let God be truly there for you, and you will see that He will come.

The Vocation Crisis

I am new to the Catholic Faith. I hear the term "vocation crisis" tossed around a good deal. What does it mean?

It means, first, the shortage of priests, seminarians, and religious brothers and sisters to do the work of the Church. It is a crisis. There has been a serious decline in the number of priests, brothers, and sisters, alongside a growth in the Catholic population. It's part of the general weakening of religion in the United States. When I was young, even in the 1950s, religion was much stronger in the United States than it is now. Part of that weakening is the loss of vocations: people leaving the priesthood or the religious life or people not coming in in the first place.

On the other hand, I'm delighted to say that, despite all the attacks of the media on religion and all the scandals and misunderstandings, despite it all, there are quite a few very fine young men and young women—and even older men and women!—coming into religious life and the priesthood. In the Catholic Church, we call them the "JP-2 generation."[81]

In our little community, we have almost twenty-five joining us this year, people who are willing to live the rest of their lives in

[81] For Pope St. John Paul II.

the slums, to work with the very poor, to wear a habit in public, to practice poverty, chastity, and obedience and long hours of prayer. Our community lives almost entirely on donated food, and it gives away hundreds of thousands of pounds of food every year. I'm hoping we'll make a million pounds a year before I check out. More are coming! You might say, "Maybe I ought to join this funny group." Where we live, in the middle of the slums, you'll never have to go to the movies for the rest of your life, because it's all around us.

The vocation crisis is caused by worldliness in the Church, and by the attacks of the media on the Catholic Church. Ann Coulter wrote a book called *Godless: The Church of Liberalism.*[82] You ought to read what she has to say about the attack of the media on the Catholic clergy. You'll find out that although the tragedy of these scandals is true, it's been puffed up, pumped up, paraded, distorted, and put completely out of proportion in order to humiliate and silence the Catholic Church. Why? Because of the Church's opposition to abortion, euthanasia, and public immorality.

[82] Crown Forum, 2006.

Women Priests?

Recently in Philadelphia, a woman reportedly offered her first Mass. This really disturbed me, as I knew there was no way this Mass could have been valid since there is no such thing as women priests. Could you elaborate on this for me?

The question of women priests was a very hot—and very understandable—question only ten years ago; I don't think it was a bad question by any means, because the role of women has changed dramatically in the last few generations. Women become prime ministers; a woman could become president of the United States. I have a friend who is a civil engineer, the mother of two children who goes out in the morning wearing her hard hat, work shoes, and blue jeans. My father was an engineer, so I can't get over this lovely young lady going out in the morning doing what my father did. It doesn't quite fit. Naturally then, the question of women becoming priests has come up.

If you understand the difference between a Protestant minister and a Catholic or Orthodox priest, then you can understand something of the Catholic Church's position on the ordination of women. A Protestant minister—and I hope I'm not offending anybody—is a person chosen and ordained by the congregation, by the body of people, there to serve them in the name of God, to lead them in prayer, to instruct and preach to them, that is, to be a teacher, preacher, counselor. A Catholic or Orthodox priest is a man accepted by the Church and called by God not to represent the people but, rather, to represent God, to represent Christ in the Holy Eucharist and in the giving of the sacraments. In other words, there are two very different understandings of the clergy. I went to the ordination of a woman friend of mine as a Presbyterian minister, but neither she, nor I, nor the minister who ordained her thought she was becoming a *Catholic* priest. Rather, we all understood that she became a *Presbyterian* minister.

Now, a woman who gets herself "ordained" to the Catholic priesthood is going directly against the ordinary teaching authority of the Church explicitly given by Pope John Paul II.[83] She's not following the rules, and so she's not a priest, and those who, for one reason or another, have encouraged her in the thought that she is, may be morally in as bad a spot as she is. In charity, I'm willing to grant that they are intrinsically confused; but even so, what they're doing is not right. It's quite wrong. Why? The decision to ordain only men to the priesthood has come through the Church; it has been this way for two thousand years. Being a good Catholic is not exactly a day off; it can be really tough. However, I do get some goodies back, one of which is the guidance of the teaching authority of the Magisterium of the Church.

[83] Apostolic Letter *Ordinatio Sacerdotalis: To the Bishops of the Catholic Church on Reserving Priestly Ordination to Men Alone* (May 22, 1994).